P9-AOT-707

# Councils of Governments:

*A Study of Political Incrementalism*

ASCUP

Nelson Wikstrom

# Councils of Governments:

*A Study of Political Incrementalism*

Nelson-Hall
Chicago

40024

**Library of Congress Cataloging in Publication Data**

Wikstrom, Nelson.
    Councils of governments.

    Bibliography: p. 145
    Includes index.
    1. Metropolitan government—United States. I. Title.
JS442.W5      352′.0094′0973      76-28784
ISBN  0-88229-322-2

Copyright © 1977 by Nelson Wikstrom.
*All rights reserved.* No part of this book may be reproduced in any form
without permission in writing from the publisher, except by a reviewer
who wishes to quote brief passages in connection with a review written
for broadcast or for inclusion in a magazine or newspaper. For
information address Nelson-Hall Inc., Publishers, 325 West Jackson
Boulevard, Chicago 60606.
*Manufactured in the United States of America.*

To
Anna and Gunnar
and
Mary, Amy, and Sara

ASOOP

# Contents

40024

# Charts

# Tables

# Preface

More than thirty years ago, Charles Merriam wrote in his preface to Victor Jones' classic work, *Metropolitan Government*, that "the adequate organization of modern metropolitan areas is one of the great unsolved problems of modern politics."[1] Merriam's dictum still holds; it is no less true today than at the juncture of time when he penned it. Indeed, it might well be stated that the question of what constitutes adequate governmental structure in our metropolitan areas has become more complex and confusing in recent times. At least, thirty years ago, there was a fairly widespread consensus that the road to urban governmental reform involved the consolidation of political units in the metropolis. After all, according to the once-dominant orthodoxy, the source of many of our urban ills could be traced back to the fragmented or decentralized political system. However, no longer does the consolidationist point of view enjoy the monopoly allegiance of scholars of urban politics, and attacks upon the consolidationist position have become increasingly numerous and more sophisticated.[2] Further, significant numbers of political scientists are arguing the case for urban political decentralization.[3] In short, the problem of what constitutes the adequate political organization of modern metropolitan areas, which Merriam noted so long ago, still remains unsolved.

We are all aware that efforts to achieve radical metropolitan political reform have generally met with failure. There are many reasons for this, not the least of which has been electorate resistance to such structural change. However, it has only been recently that scholars of urban politics have begun to realize the importance and significance of incremental political change in the metropolis. H. Paul Friesema has documented, at least in the metropolitan area that served as the focus of his research, that there is far more cooperation than chaos between local governments than we have been led to believe.[4] Other scholars have found similar cooperation in other metropolitan areas. Joseph F. Zimmerman has inventoried and documented the numerous local horizontal intergovernmental agreements and contracts in the United States.[5] In a very real sense, the sorry record of radical metropolitan reform has been in part responsible for ushering in a period of massive cooperation between governmental units in the metropolis.

This volume is concerned with the council of governments device and its role in promoting incremental political change in the metropolis. This work addresses itself to (1) the definition of what a council of governments is *and what it is not*, (2) an overview of council development and factors supporting this development, (3) the formation and structural attributes of councils, (4) council activities and functions, (5) questions of immediate and long-range concern relating to councils, and (6) the significance of councils of governments in the metropolitan political world. It is the contention of the author that massive, governmental, structural reform is neither needed nor desired in the American metropolis, since councils provide an ideal, responsible, democratic mechanism for program coordination, policy direction, and management in the metropolis, as Royce Hanson noted in the late sixties.[6]

Despite the proliferation of councils of governments— there are now about 450 councils in the United States— *relatively* little scholarly concern has been devoted to councils and council development. This volume is designed to, hopefully, partially fill this intellectual void. The assertions and overall findings set forth are based on a comprehensive review of the appropriate literature and field interviews conducted with local political elites and those immediately involved in council activity.

The potential audience for this work is large and varied. Students enrolled in urban politics and intergovernmental relations courses, especially at the graduate level, will find this work presents a well-developed alternative to the more familiar consolidationist point of view. Practitioners of government, especially those employed by councils and other regional organizations, can read this book with profit. The layman who wishes to read a serious discourse on urban government will find this work interesting and informative.

I wish to thank all those—in academe and in the field—who aided me in the preparation of this volume. Their comments and insights on councils of governments immeasurably added to my understanding of these bodies. Walter Scheiber, Executive Director of the Metropolitan Washington Council of Governments, was especially generous in taking time out of his active schedule to converse several times with me about the council approach. Mikki Dudley receives my sincere thanks for typing several drafts of the manuscript and putting up with my assorted scholarly demands. Finally, I thank my wife, Mary, and my daughter, Amy, for their patience and understanding while I was preparing this volume. A husband and father engaged in writing a manuscript can often be more self-centered than he realizes.

# Notes

1. Charles E. Merriam, preface to Victor Jones, *Metropolitan Government* (Chicago: University of Chicago Press, 1942), p. ix.
2. See, for instance, Robert L. Bish and Vincent Ostrom, *Understanding Urban Government: Metropolitan Reform Reconsidered* (Washington, D.C.: American Enterprise Institute for Public Policy Research, 1973).
3. See, for example, Alan A. Altshuler, *Community Control: The Black Demand for Participation in Large American Cities* (New York: Pegasus, 1970), and Milton Kotler, *Neighborhood Government: The Local Foundations of Political Life* (New York: Bobbs-Merrill, 1969).
4. H. Paul Friesema, *Metropolitan Political Structure: Intergovernmental Relations and Political Integration in the Quad-Cities* (Iowa City: University of Iowa Press, 1971).
5. Joseph F. Zimmerman, "Meeting Service Needs through Intergovernmental Agreements," in *The Municipal Yearbook, 1973* (Washington, D.C.: International City Management Association, 1973), pp. 79-88.
6. Royce Hanson, "The Council of Governments—What Is It?" (Paper delivered at the First National Conference on Councils of Governments, Washington, D.C., April 2, 1967), p. 2.

# The Metropolitan Governmental Mosaic  1

The emergence of metropolitan America has ushered in an era of critical or not-so-critical, depending upon one's perspective, urban problems.[1] These problems are quite diverse and varied; some relate to the very maintenance and "worthiness" of the American economic, political, and social system itself. For example, much has been written on the supposed plight and lack of opportunity for those members of minority groups, chiefly blacks, who languish in the "cellar" of American society and who fail to receive in any proportional way the rewards of the American system.

In contrast to the broad societal problem cited above, many of the problems that confront urban America are quite specific and can be readily discerned and identified. These more "narrow" problems may be, as the late Paul Studenski has aptly pointed out, essentially divided into two categories. On the one hand, there are those classified as "particular service problems."[2] Included in this category are such items as the lack of decent and adequate housing, juvenile delinquency and crime in general, air and water pollution, vehicle-traffic congestion, antiquated mass-transit systems, substandard public schools, and inadequate parks and other recreational areas.

## Fragmented Urban Government

Notwithstanding the problems cited above, none of which should be minimized or discounted, the most fundamental problem of the metropolis according to many social scientists is what Studenski has repeatedly referred to as one of a basic "organizational nature,"[3] that is, the "fractional" or "fragmented" character of government in urban areas. In 1972, according to the authoritative *Census of Governments* issued by the U.S. Bureau of the Census, there were no less than 22,185 local governmental bodies in 264 metropolitan areas.[4] In each of our urban areas there are usually numerous municipalities, special districts, authorities, counties, and other varied governmental units. Robert Wood, in a study sponsored by the Regional Plan Association of New York, identified 1,467 governmental bodies in the New York region in the latter part of the fifties.[5] The Chicago metropolis is not far behind: presently it is endowed with 1,172 governmental bodies.[6] One has good reason to agree with Studenski's claim that there is in the typical metropolis a ". . . basic disparity between the disunified nature of the political and administrative organization of such an area and its relatively unified social and economic structure. . . ."[7]

Our real concern is not with simply the abundance of governmental bodies in metropolitan areas; rather, it is the notion, conveyed by many, that a good share of the ills of urban life have their origin or genesis in the decentralized nature of the metropolitan political system.[8] Luther Gulick, in his work, *The Metropolitan Problem and American Ideas*, states that failures directly attributed to the "fragmented" nature of government in the metropolis include a lack or inadequate amount of services and the absence of a comprehensive program for general development and for tackling major economic and social problems on a metropolitan basis. Further, Gulick asserts that governmental "decentralization" is at least partly responsible for the lack of metropolitan leadership:

> [There is a] lack of region-wide democratic machinery for teamwork, for thinking about and dealing with the common problems of the metropolitan area. This is important because, without such machinery, the people who live in the metropolitan areas cannot rise up, develop plans for action, debate proposals, iron out acceptable compromises, and then agree to join hands and take action. Without such teamwork machinery, there is no constituency, no sense of common purpose, no "metropolitan community" in a political sense, and, what is all important, no "metropolitan leadership."[9]

Whether or not the decentralized character of the metropolitan political system is, to a large extent, the source of urban problems cannot be conclusively stated. The traditional, or "consolidationist" interpretation, which places great emphasis on the pattern of municipal fiscal disparities resultant of metropolitan political fragmentation, would seem to indicate thus. Yet some scholars of urban politics have cast doubts on its validity. Brett Hawkins and Thomas Dye found that metropolitan political fragmentation bears no relationship to governmental spending for municipal services nor, by implication, to the quality of municipal services. They assert, "Our point is that metropolitan 'fragmentation,' as well as reorganization and centralization, must be examined primarily in terms of the socio-economic values involved, rather than their public service or spending consequences. Evidently the service argument against fragmentation has been used in error."[10] Jewell Bellish, in an issue of the *National Civic Review* published some years ago, reminded us that "those who have urged some form of metropolitan governmental system have never empirically proven that fragmented institutional arrangements have been the cause of the unresolved problems."[11] Further, several students of urban politics, identified with the "public-choice" school of thought, maintain that in terms of meeting the varied priority needs of citizens, a decentralized metropolitan political system is preferable to that of one of a unified character.[12] In addition, exponents of the community control or neighborhood government approach assert that the fundamental political problem of the metropolis is not too many governments, but too few.[13] In a very real sense, it seems clear that the existence of decentralized metropolitan government has served as a catalyst of reform—governmental structural reform sought by reformers who believe that the metropolitan political system is incapable of coping with the multitude of burdens and tasks placed upon it. We now turn to a summary survey of these metropolitan consolidation governmental structural changes.

## One-Government Approach

Metropolitan consolidation governmental structural reorganizational proposals can be divided into two general types.[14] First are those proposals that stress the necessity of one comprehensive government—the so-called one-government approach—for the entire metropolitan area. This one metropolitanwide governmental body would supply virtually all essential services for the inhabitants of the region. Municipal governments and other governmental units would simply be dispensed with. Other governmental consolidation reorganizational proposals are predicated upon the assumption that the political system of the metropolis should be "federal" in character; that is, whereas some functions and services would continue to be delivered by municipal and other local governmental bodies, services of an area-wide, or regional, nature would be the province of the metropolitan government.

Two basic "tools" have been employed by reformers of the one governmental persuasion to realize their objective: annexation and city-county consolidation. One "tool" has been relatively successful, but limited; the other has been, to a large extent, of limited utility. Annexation has been skillfully employed in the recent past by some core cities, primarily in the South and Southwest, to increase their hegemony; through this device, Oklahoma City at one period in the 1960's enjoyed the distinction of being, in terms of land area, the largest city in the world.[15] Also, Atlanta, Houston, and Dallas by annexation have significantly enlarged their boundaries. Yet the most important factor accounting for their annexation success—the fact that each of these cities was largely surrounded by *unincorporated* land areas—has limited the utility of this consolidation strategy in other metropolitan areas. Where great core cities are usually surrounded by incorporated municipal neighbors, such as in the East, the "tool" of annexation, though widely resorted to by these cities in the nineteenth century, has not been a *recent* viable political alternative in the quest for metropolitan government, as the record well reveals.[16]

As indicated above, reformers of metropolitan governmental structure have employed, where annexation was seemingly not a viable or preferred alternative, the strategy of city-county consolidation to realize their goal of comprehensive metropolitan government. Generally, this method has met with repeated failure; proponents have suffered defeats, to cite but a few examples, in the metropolitan areas of Knoxville, Tennessee; Macon, Georgia; and St. Louis, Missouri.[17] Vincent Marando reminds us that for every successful city-county consolidation attempt, there have been three rejections.[18] Nevertheless, we should note that city-county consolidation efforts have been realized in the metropolitan regions of Baton Rouge (in 1947),[19] Nashville (in 1962),[20] Jacksonville (in 1967),[21] and Indianapolis (in 1969).[22]

## "Federal" Metropolitan Government

Due to the limited utility and political feasibility of the one-government approach to reorganizing the political system of the metropolis (two scholars of urban politics have stated that ". . . the one-government approach to area-wide problems has passed its heyday"[23]), reformers have set forth reorganizational proposals of a "federal" character. Metropolitan governmental reorganization proposals based on "federalism" have simply meant this: public services and functions of an area-wide import would be delivered by a regional-wide government body, while those of a local orientation would remain the province of the municipal governments. While philosophically the concept of a "federal" metropolitan government is lucid, in political practice it has been difficult discerning and identifying exactly which functions and services are the domain of each level of government.[24]

Efforts to reconstitute the governmental structure of the metropolis along the lines of "federalism" have met, generally, with failure. Attempts by reformers to seek a "federal" political system in the metropolitan areas of Pittsburgh, Houston, Dayton (Ohio), and Cleveland have been defeated by the electorate. Indeed, in the latter community, reformers have suffered numerous defeats.[25] In the United States, only in the Miami-Dade County metropolitan region has a "federal" system been established; even in this instance, the plan has been under unceasing attack, as the literature well indicates.[26] Less controversial has been the adoption and operation of the federal metropolitan government of Toronto, Canada, which began functioning in 1954.[27]

## Community Control
## and Neighborhood Government

In direct contrast to those reformers who have advocated the desirability of an area-wide consolidated metropolitan government, others have articulated the need to decentralize the entire political system and establish governments at the neighborhood level. Milton Kotler, in his volume *Neighborhood Government,* asserts that the *major* political problem of the metropolis is the loss of political liberty and the consequent political estrangement and alienation suffered primarily by the minorities and disadvantaged of core cities.[28] Kotler argues that only with the establishment of neighborhood government can these citizens enjoy political liberty and self-rule, and gain a sense of control over their own political destiny. Such neighborhood governments would provide their constituents with education, health, safety, and welfare services. In addition, Alan Altshuler, another exponent of the neighborhood government concept, maintains that the establishment of neighborhood government would enhance black political development and promote racial peace.[29] Although advocates of neighborhood government have failed to realize the establishment of these governmental units, there has been a trend in large core cities toward municipal administrative decentralization.[30]

## Failure of
## Major Metro Efforts

What accounts for the failure of consolidationist reformers of the metropolitan political system (Scott Greer

7

writes: "The results have been failure, in city after city, time after time."[31]) to realize their objectives? The design and purpose of this study are not centrally concerned with this issue, but a few reasons and speculations will be advanced concerning electorate resistance to reform proposals. Greer has asserted that the basic factor contributing to defeat has been the underlying cultural norms held by Americans concerning local government (i.e., government closest to the people is the best government) and the resulting political and governmental systems built upon them.[32] More specifically, it appears that the prime reason for the pattern of failure is the fundamental belief held by a majority of the electorate that there is no need for an area-wide governmental structure in the metropolis. Marando has written about city-county consolidation attempts: "City-county consolidations do not spring from the desires of a broad base of the population. The benefits of consolidated government appear too abstract or too long range for the immediate interests of the voter."[33] Similarly, John Bollens has noted in a more general fashion:

> Experienced observers of the metropolitan scene may be acutely aware of the defects and potential dangers that lie in the present system, but the average citizen has little such consciousness. He may be dissatisfied with the performance of certain functions, he may desire better or additional services, he may wonder at times where all this explosive growth is leading and what it means in terms of his daily living, but he is not deeply troubled. He feels no impelling need, no urgency, for any major restructuring of the governmental pattern of the area.[34]

Robert Wood asserts that reform proposals are defeated because they disturb the political status quo and raise more questions than they provide solutions:

> By ignoring the effects of their proposals on existing power structures, by failing to set an alternative and better political process as a goal, and most of all by slightly individual values, advocates of annexation, consolidation, or even

federation thus raise insuperable problems of representation and shifts in political influence.

## Elaborating on the above, Wood conjectures:

In effect, they (the reformers) demand sizeable surrenders of local privileges and prerogatives in return for promises of administrative benefits. There is small assurance that the new political process, designed usually to provide for indirect representation or to refurbish a county government long in disrepute, will protect the individual's interest in customary ways or enhance his capacity to participate in the vital decisions of the region. All that is clear is that functions are moving upstairs to a "greater government," undefined and unknown in its political balance, while the localities are to be left such challenging tasks as the erection of street signs and traffic lights, tree care, and the celebration of holidays.

## Wood reminds the reader:

Questions of procedure and process, of how local communities might influence the politics of the larger government, of how they might retain options with respect to the conduct of activities in their areas, of how flexible administration was to be assured, were largely ignored. Elegant skeletons of government spring forth, but the capacity to govern subject to regularized restraints is missing.[35]

Finally, governmental reform proposals for the metropolis have suffered an ill fate for they are predicated upon values that are seemingly not widely shared by the entire community. For instance, Edward C. Banfield reminds us that "the idea that there are values, such as efficiency, which pertain to the community as a whole and to which the private interests of individuals ought to be subordinated, has never impressed the working-class voter."[36]

### Intergovernmental Cooperation

Although attempts to restructure the government of the metropolis have usually ended in failure, one should not surmise from this that the exclusive political denominator of urban political life is conflict; there is conflict, to be sure, but there is also cooperation. Extensive horizontal cooperation between governmental units in the metropolis does exist, more so than is commonly acknowledged and discerned; indeed, it is the lack of a formal metropolitan governmental structure that, to a large extent, is responsible for increased voluntary cooperation among governmental units in American urban areas.[37]

Cooperation among governmental jurisdictions in the metropolis takes varied forms; the two most basic types are mere consultation between municipal officials and the use of contractual arrangements. As the late Karl Bosworth wrote some years ago, public officials, through collective consultation and the employment of contractual arrangements, have been able, in pursuit of their goals, to circumvent institutional barriers:

> Wherever one has talked with local governmental officials over the past several decades he has found that they have ways of consulting among themselves across jurisdictional boundaries. . . . Informal and contractual arrangements have been the common way of rising above the problems of multiple governments, whether the problem is the maintenance of a boundary river bridge, the collaboration of fire or police forces, or the expression of a common view among local officials of a region on some state legislative issues affecting the area.[38]

Horizontal contractual arrangements of a functional and service character among governmental units are the most salient examples of local intergovernmental cooperation. There is evidence supporting the belief that horizontal contractual agreements were employed by local governmental units as long ago as the colonial period.[39] Studenski found that, in the 1930's, contractual agreements were utilized in the following areas: the construction of bridges, the construction and maintenance of sewers, the construction of parkways, the enforcement of uniform traffic regulations, the establishment of bus routes and franchises, general law enforcement, and the sale of water by the central city to suburbanites.[40]

Current examples of functional contractual arrangements among local governments in the metropolis can be classified into three general varieties: (1) a single government performs a service or provides a facility for one or more other local units, (2) two or more local governments perform a function jointly or operate a facility on a joint basis, and, (3) two or more local governments assist or supply mutual aid to one another in emergency situations, such as a large fire. Most of these contractual arrangements are of the latter type. Examples of municipal services delivered on a contractual basis include fire and police protection, library services, and public health programs.[41]

Although wide use has been made of contractual arrangements in many metropolitan areas, including Philadelphia, Cleveland, and St. Louis, contracts have been employed to the greatest extent in the burgeoning metropolis of Los Angeles. The County of Los Angeles provides such services as law enforcement and traffic signals to densely populated unincorporated areas. In addition, the County, under what has become popularly known as the "Lakewood Plan," supplies municipalities with such functions as election services, enforcement of city health ordinances, library services, engineering services, law enforcement, and fire protection. Indeed, some of the municipalities of the areas obtain practically all of their services from the county.[42]

Despite the widespread and seemingly satisfactory operation of contractual arrangements among local governments, several scholars have questioned the advisability of their employment. Joseph F. Zimmerman notes that the proliferation of contracts may have three disadvantages:

First, the average citizen may experience greater difficulty in understanding a local government system made more complex by the widespread use of multilateral agreements and he may be unable to pinpoint responsibility for failures in the system. Second, agreements may reinforce the existing fragmented governmental system in the typical metropolitan area and reduce pressures for creation of an area-wide government with adequate powers to solve metropolitan major problems. A third and related disadvantage is the possible promotion of additional political fractionation and fiscal disparities.[43]

Joseph Small, advancing some observations similar to those of Zimmerman, has enumerated what he believes are the negative features of such arrangements:

. . . Some services involve policies that will be welcomed by some municipalities and opposed by others. . . .

A network of intergovernmental agreements tends to confuse the lines of responsibility, and the voter along with his local city council may have lost the control he sought to retain.

. . . A series of particular contracts for individual services makes it difficult for residents and local officials to appreciate the whole picture of area-wide needs. . . .

Another weakness has been the rush to incorporate previously unorganized communities. There is a point beyond which the creation of new municipalities in a given area becomes a deterrent to orderly government. . . .

Finally, whenever there is a buyer and a seller, there is the possibility of a monopoly with the seller overcharging the buyer who has nowhere else to go and who cannot afford to organize the services alone. On the other hand, in a long term contract conditions may arise that prevent the seller from getting a fair return. . . .[44]

Whatever may be the advantages and limitations of contractual arrangements, they will remain a permanent feature of the urban political scene. After all, it is only through such arrangements that many of the public needs of the inhabitants are met and satisfied.

## Voluntary Associations
## of Public Officials

Although contractual arrangements are the most structural and visible example of local intergovernmental cooperation in the metropolis, one should not discount the value of mere consultation among locally elected officials and the associations brought into being to promote this consultation. Voluntary associations of elected officials have long been a part of the American scene. Initially, to any real meaningful and significant extent, these associations of local officials were of a state-wide orientation; some years after the state organizations made their appearance, national organizations of a similar character and purpose were formed. And, based on the associational concept, there soon arose in a number of American urban areas conferences, or associations, of *local* governmental officials.

Associations of local governmental officials were first organized on a state-wide and national basis before the turn of the present century. The Indiana Municipal League was established in 1891. Soon thereafter, similar organizations were formed in Iowa (1889), California (1898), Wisconsin (1898), Michigan (1899), and Illinois (1899). Over the years, these types of organizations have continued to increase in number; presently there are no less than forty-two state municipal leagues of local officials. The League of American Municipalities, formed in 1897, represented the first instance of a nationwide association of cities. It was subsequently joined by its counterpart, the American Municipal Association (now the National League of Cities), whose initial and continuing purpose is to give large cities, represented by their mayors, a means by which they could discuss matters of common concern and agree on future action and policy.[45]

The above organizations have generally proved to be meaningful and resourceful entities for informing local officials about various matters and promoting cooperation among them and their respective governments. As one distinguished scholar of urban affairs has stated:

> The leagues and associations of cities from the beginning provided for some clearing-house functions on current problems and practices. These have been developed materially and have also been supplemented by various consultant services to members, co-operative activities, e.g., centralized purchasing for smaller municipalities and training courses for municipal employees, co-operative research and publication, usually with university or college bureaus of municipal research, that cover problems of increasing range and complexity.[46]

## Development of Regional Conferences

Notwithstanding the importance of the above organizations for promoting local intergovernmental cooperation, this work is primarily concerned with the development of *regional* associations of a similar nature and intent. Studenski, writing in the early thirties, informs us that, even as early as that period, there were regional associations or conferences of local officials and other interested parties designed to promote greater metropolitan understanding and common action functioning in several metropolitan areas:

> In a few instances intermunicipal conferences have been organized with purely advisory functions. They may be composed exclusively of city officials or partly of officials and partly of citizens or representatives of civic organizations. Such conferences may concern themselves with general matters of metropolitan character or may confine their attention to a single specified subject. Their deliberations may give rise to inter-city undertakings of metropolitan character.[47]

Examples of these regional conferences included a metropolitan council of elected officials in the Cleveland area, an association of police chiefs in the northern New Jersey region, and metropolitan-planning conferences organized in the Buffalo, Los Angeles, and Minneapolis-St. Paul urban environs.[48] Several characteristics of these associations or conferences should be noted here. First, they were simply advisory and voluntary bodies; i.e., they possessed no substantive functions and/or powers. Second, with the exception of the Cleveland council, each was concerned largely with one particular function and not with all of the known problems of the metropolis. Why the latter was true has been well answered by Victor Jones: "The least formal of intergovernmental arrangements arises out of the daily contacts of local officials and other individuals interested in a *particular* [italics mine] problem. These contacts are often very casual. . . ."[49] Hence, to a very large extent, the participants of initial regional associations were like individuals pursuing a similar, albeit often technical, vocation.

To be sure, the early conference approach for coping with metropolitan problems had a limited utility. In evaluating this mechanism Studenski wrote:

> . . . Cooperation has helped, here and there, in some metropolitan areas to meet particular situations, or to promote comprehensive arrangements for solving metropolitan problems. But it has not succeeded in unifying the government of a metropolitan area sufficiently to make possible the comprehensive and effective solving of the metropolitan problem.[50]

To suggest that the early conference approach had a limited utility is not to imply that it is an undesirable approach for seeking cooperative action among local governments in the metropolis; quite the converse is true, as Jones well assures us:

> It is possible, however, and often desirable to bring people interested in a common problem into a conference. Such

meetings can easily become a waste of time but, they are also an effective means of communication if they are skillfully led and if the information to be used in the discussion has been assembled and organized before the meeting.[51]

## From Conferences to
## Metropolitan Councils of Elected Officials

Based on the conference mechanism, cooperation between local governments in the metropolis has been facilitated through a relatively new institution—metropolitan councils or conferences of governments; popularly referred to as COGs. Many scholars of the urban scene view the council device with considerable optimism. As long ago as 1966, Henry J. Schmandt wrote: "The creation of metropolitan or regional councils has been one of the most promising developments in recent years."[52] Jones, one of the most prolific writers on the device, stated in 1962: "I view voluntary metropolitan associations of local governments . . . as the most promising development in our American federal system."[53] Numerous others have referred to the council device in favorable terms.[54]

### Councils of Governments—What Are They?

Exactly what is a metropolitan council or conference of governments? The definition advanced by Norman Beckman some years ago is still appropriate:

> These are voluntary associations of elected public officials from most or all of the governments of a metropolitan area, formed to develop a consensus regarding metropolitan needs and actions to be taken in solving their problems.[55]

A report submitted to the Governor of Texas elaborates on this definition:

> It is *voluntary* because no local government has to join, and any local government may withdraw.

It is an *association* because it has no power to tax or incur debt and does not possess the police powers essential to a true government.

It represents *governments* as political entities; it does *not* represent people except as they are represented through their local governments [italics in original].[56]

What should be realized is a council of governments is not in general parlance a "government"; specifically, it is not a "metropolitan government." Nor should it be necessarily analyzed as a structure designed to prevent "metropolitan government" from coming into being; conversely, it is not determinately the first stage toward realization of "metropolitan government." And, it is certainly not, nor intended to be, a panacea that will solve all of the known problems of the metropolis. Finally, although the focus of this work concerns councils of governments in metropolitan areas it should be recognized that there are numerous councils functioning in nonurban regions.

There are about 450 councils of governments in the United States.[57] Despite the proliferation and popularity of the council mechanism, councils of governments are somewhat of an intellectual enigma.[58] Open questions include the following: How, and for what reasons, do councils come into existence? Which individuals and groups involved in urban politics promote and support, and conversely which disapprove of and oppose, the council mechanism? What issues and problems concern council members? What do these bodies contemplate and eventually perform in a substantive fashion? What are the supposed limitations of the council approach and councils? What is the nature of council leadership? Can one discern a pattern of development for councils? What is the present and future significance of councils of governments in the larger metropolitan political process?

In an attempt to provide at least partial answers to the

above and related questions, the author gathered information on the council experience through a review of the appropriate literature and field interviews; particular attention was devoted to the following ten councils or conferences of governments: (1) Association of Bay Area Governments (San Francisco), (2) Metropolitan Atlanta Council of Local Governments,[59] (3)Metropolitan Washington Council of Governments, (4) Mid-Willamette Valley Council of Governments (Salem, Oregon), (5) Puget Sound Governmental Conference (Seattle-Tacoma), (6) Regional Conference of Elected Officials (Philadelphia),[60] (7) Southern California Association of Governments (Los Angeles), (8) Supervisors' Inter-County Committee and its successor, the Southeast Michigan Council of Governments (Detroit), and (9) Capitol Region Council of Elected Officials (Hartford, Connecticut).[61]

In addition, this study includes data obtained by the author some years ago in Connecticut from extensive survey research that was designed to ascertain the attitude of selected individuals involved in the political process toward the council device. The components of the sample included Democratic and Republican party local chairmen, elected public officials (mayors and first selectmen), and city or town managers in three generally defined regional areas—Hartford, New Haven, and Norwich-New London. Empirical data generated from this survey and information acquired on the council experience in general constitute the factual information from which are advanced some conclusions and generalizations about councils of governments.

# Notes

1. For contrasting views concerning the severity of our urban problems, see Mitchell Gordon, *Sick Cities: Psychology and Pathology of American Urban Life* (Baltimore: Penguin Books, 1963) and Edward C. Banfield, *The Unheavenly City Revisited* (Boston: Little, Brown and Company, 1974).
2. Paul Studenski, "Metropolitan Areas 1960," *National Civic Review* 49 (October 1960): 468.
3. Ibid.
4. U.S., Bureau of the Census, *Census of Governments, 1972,* vol. 1, *Governmental Organization* (Washington, D.C.: Government Printing Office, 1973), p. 10.
5. Robert Wood, *1400 Governments* (Garden City, N.Y.: Doubleday, Anchor Books, 1964), p. 1.
6. U.S., Bureau of the Census, *Census of Governments, 1972,* p. 152.
7. Studenski, "Metropolitan Areas 1960," p. 468.
8. For illustrative literature supporting this view, see Paul Studenski, *The Government of Metropolitan Areas* (New York: National Municipal League, 1930) and Victor Jones, *Metropolitan Government* (Chicago: University of Chicago Press, 1942), especially pp. 52-84. A good summary of this consolidationist point of view is found in Robert O. Warren, *Government in Metropolitan Regions: A Reappraisal of Fractionated Political Organization* (Davis, Calif.: Institute of Governmental Affairs University of California, 1966), pp. 5-17.
9. Luther Gulick, *The Metropolitan Problem and American Ideas* (New York: Knopf, 1962), p. 123. See the author's article, "Metropolitan Organization," *Annals of the American Academy of Political and Social Science* 314 (November 1957): 57-65, for additional material supporting his analysis.
10. Brett Hawkins and Thomas R. Dye, "Metropolitan 'Fragmentation': A Research Note," *American Behavioral Scientist* 5 (May 1962): 11.
11. Jewell Bellish, review of *Government in Metropolitan Regions: A Reappraisal of Fractionated Political Organization* by Robert O. Warren, *National Civic Review* 56 (February 1966): 119.

12. Representative of this position is Robert L. Bish and Vincent Ostrom's, *Understanding Urban Government: Metropolitan Reform Reconsidered* (Washington, D.C.: American Enterprise Institute for Public Policy Research, 1973).

13. See, for example, Alan A. Altshuler, *Community Control: The Black Demand for Participation in Large American Cities* (New York: Pegasus, 1970) and Milton Kotler, *Neighborhood Government: The Local Foundations of Political Life* (New York: Bobbs-Merrill, 1969).

14. For introductory literature on the politics of metropolitan reform, see Advisory Commission on Intergovernmental Relations, *Factors Affecting Voter Reactions to Governmental Reorganization in Metropolitan Areas* (Washington, D.C.: The Commission, 1962); Scott Greer, *Governing the Metropolis* (New York: Wiley, 1962), pp. 119-128, and by the same author, *Metropolitics: A Study of Political Culture* (New York: Wiley, 1963); Edward C. Banfield, "The Politics of Metropolitan Area Organization," *Midwest Journal of Political Science* 1 (May 1957): 77-91; Bernard J. Frieden, *Metropolitan America: Challenge to Federalism* (Washington, D.C.: Advisory Commission on Intergovernmental Relations, 1966), pp. 107-110; and, Joseph F. Zimmerman, "Metropolitan Reform in the U.S.: An Overview," *Public Administration Review* 30 (September/October 1970): 531-543.

15. Gordon, *Sick Cities,* p. 367.

16. On this point, see John Bollens and Henry J. Schmandt, *The Metropolis: Its People, Politics, and Economic Life* (New York: Harper and Row, 1965), p. 433. For additional evidence see Thomas R. Dye, "Urban Political Integration: Conditions Associated with Annexation in American Cities," *Midwest Journal of Political Science* 8 (November 1964): 430-445.

17. For reasons of defeat in St. Louis, see Carl A. McCandless, "Metro Charter Campaign Fails," *National Civic Review* 49 (February 1960): 91-93; Robert H. Salisbury, "The Dynamics of Reform: Charter Politics in St. Louis," *Midwest Journal of Political Science* 5 (August 1960): 474-484; and Henry J. Schmandt, Paul G. Steinbicker, and George Wendel, *Metropolitan Reform in St. Louis* (New York: Holt, Rinehart, and Winston, 1961).

18. Vincent Marando, "The Politics of City-County Consolidation," *National Civic Review* 64 (February 1975): 76. For further analysis, see also by the same author, "Voting in City-County Consolidation," *Western Political Quarterly* 26 (March 1973): 90-96.

19. See William C. Havard, Jr. and Floyd L. Corty, *Rural-Urban Consolidation* (Baton Rouge, La.: Louisiana State University Press, 1964).

20. See Daniel R. Grant, "Urban and Suburban Nashville: A Case Study in Metropolitanism," *Journal of Politics* 17 (February 1955): 82-99, and by the same author, "Metropolitics and Professional Political Leadership: The Case of Nashville," *Annals of the American Academy of Political and Social Science* 353 (May 1964): 72-83. Also, see David Booth, *Metropolitics: The Nashville Consolidation* (East Lansing, Mich.: Institute for Community Development and Services, Michigan State University, 1963), and Brett Hawkins, "Public Opinion and Metropolitan Reorganization in Nashville," *Journal of Politics* 28 (May 1966): 408-418.

21. See Richard A. Martin, *Consolidation: Jacksonville-Duval County* (Jacksonville: Crawford Publishing Co., 1968).

22. See York Willbern, "Unigov: Local Government Reorganization in Indianapolis," in *The Regionalist Papers*, ed. Kent Mathewson (Detroit: Metropolitan Fund, 1974), pp. 207-229.

23. Bollens and Schmandt, *The Metropolis*, p. 438.

24. The Advisory Commission on Intergovernmental Relations has developed a set of economic and political criteria for determining whether functions should be carried out at the local or regional level. See their publication, *Performance of Urban Functions: Local and Area-Wide* (Washington, D.C.: The Commission, 1963).

25. See James A. Norton, *The Metro Experience* (Cleveland: Western Reserve University Press, 1963), and by the same author, "Referenda Voting in a Metropolitan Area," *Western Political Science Quarterly* 16 (March 1963): 195-212.

26. See Edward Sofen, *The Miami Metropolitan Experiment* (Bloomington, Indiana: Indiana University Press, 1963), and by the same author, "The Problems of Metropolitan Leadership: The Miami Experience," *Midwest Journal of Political Science* 5 (February 1961): 18-38.

27. See Harold Kaplan, *Urban Political Systems: A Functional Analysis of Metro Toronto* (New York: Columbia University Press, 1967).

28. Kotler, *Neighborhood Government*, p. 39.

29. Altshuler, *Community Control*, p. 201.

30. See Joseph F. Zimmerman, *The Federated City: Community Control in Large Cities* (New York: St. Martin's Press, 1972), especially pp. 41-64.

31. Greer, *Governing the Metropolis*, p. 122.

32. Ibid., p. 124.

33. Marando, "The Politics of City-County Consolidation," p. 81.

34. John C. Bollens, ed., *Exploring the Metropolitan Community* (Berkeley, Calif.: University of California Press, 1961), p. 70.

35. Robert C. Wood, "A Division of Powers in Metropolitan Areas," in *Area and Power*, ed., Arthur Maass (Glencoe, Ill: The Free Press, 1959), pp. 63-64.

36. Banfield, "The Politics of Metropolitan Area Organization," p. 90.

37. For an excellent study of intergovernmental cooperation in the Quad-City metropolitan area of Illinois and Iowa see, H. Paul Friesema, *Metropolitan Political Structure: Intergovernmental Relations and Political Integration in the Quad-Cities* (Iowa City: University of Iowa Press, 1971).

38. Karl Bosworth and Nelson Wikstrom, *Regional Councils of Elected Officials in Connecticut* (Storrs, Conn.: Institute of Urban Research, The University of Connecticut, 1966), p. 1.

39. Joseph F. Zimmerman, "Meeting Service Needs through Intergovernmental Agreements," in *The Municipal Yearbook, 1973* (Washington, D.C.: International City Management Association, 1973), p. 79.

40. Studenski, *The Government of Metropolitan Areas*, pp. 43-64.

41. This brief discussion of the nature of current contractual arrangements is based largely on Bollens and Schmandt, *The Metropolis*, pp. 371-392. See also the excellent description pertaining to this subject matter in Chapter XXI, "Interlocal Relations," of W. Brooke Graves, *American Intergovernmental Relations* (New York: Charles Scribner's Sons, 1964), pp. 737-779. For a fairly recent exhaustive inventory of intergovernmental agreements see, Zimmerman, "Meeting Service Needs through Intergovernmental Agreements," pp. 79-88.

42. For an informed analysis on how the "Lakewood Plan" came into being, see Warren, *Government in Metropolitan Regions,* pp. 141-161. A negative analysis of the "Plan" is provided by Richard M. Coin, "Accommodation Par Excellence: The Lakewood Plan," in *Metropolitan Politics,* ed., Michael N. Danielson, (Boston: Little, Brown and Company, 1966), pp. 272-280.
43. Joseph F. Zimmerman, "The Metropolitan Area Problem," *The Annals of the American Academy of Political and Social Science,* 416 (November 1974): 145-146.
44. Joseph Small, *Governmental Alternatives Facing the Chicago Metropolitan Area* (Chicago: Center for Research in Urban Government, Loyola University, 1966), p. 13.
45. Material for this paragraph was drawn largely from Coleman Woodbury, "The Background and Prospects of Urban Redevelopment in the United States," in *The Future of Cities and Urban Redevelopment,* ed., Coleman Woodbury (Chicago: University of Chicago Press, 1953), pp. 675-676.
46. Ibid., p. 676.
47. Studenski, *The Government of Metropolitan Areas,* p. 52.
48. Ibid., pp. 52-53.
49. Victor Jones, "Local Government Organization in Metropolitan Areas: Its Relation to Urban Redevelopment," in Woodbury, *The Future of Cities and Urban Redevelopment,* p. 533.
50. Studenski, *The Government of Metropolitan Areas,* p. 54.
51. Jones, "Local Government Organization in Metropolitan Areas," p. 533.
52. Henry J. Schmandt, "The Emerging Strategy," *National Civic Review* 55 (June 1966): 325.
53. Victor Jones, "Cooperative Pattern," *National Civic Review* 51 (June 1962): 308.
54. For example, Richard H. Leach wrote in the early sixties: "Metropolitan problems and the problems of intergovernmental relations that compound them are far from inseparable—and they need not be solved exclusively from either the state capitol or from Washington—if local administrators in other metropolitan areas would avail themselves of the kind of self-help [a council of governments], which has proven its worth in the giant metropolitan areas of Detroit, Washington, and New York, and more recently in San

Francisco." See, "New Urban Challenge," *National Civic Review* 50 (October 1961): 518.

55. Norman Beckman, "Alternative Approaches for Metropolitan Reorganization," *Public Management* 46 (June 1964): 130.

56. The Texas Research League, *Metropolitan Texas: A Workable Approach to Its Problems* (Austin, Tex.: The League, 1967), p. 46.

57. Interview with Ralph Webster of the National Association of Regional Councils, Washington, D.C., June 20, 1974.

58. However, one should note that the Advisory Commission on Intergovernmental Relations in their study of substate regionalism accumulated a substantial body of data on councils of governments; I have incorporated some of their material into this study. See, in particular, *Regional Decision Making: New Strategies for Substate Districts* (Washington, D.C.: The Commission, 1973).

59. Succeeded by the Atlanta Regional Commission in 1971.

60. Activities assumed by the Delaware Valley Regional Planning Commission established in 1965.

61. Merged with the Capitol Region Planning Agency, 1974.

40024

# The Rise and Proliferation of Councils of Governments 2

The number of councils of governments established over the past twenty years is impressive. In fact, the council movement may well be characterized as one that began as a "trickle" in the mid-fifties and turned into a "flood" during the period 1965-70. The rapidity of the movement caught many scholars of regionalism and urban politics "off-guard."[1] The first council of governments, the Supervisor's Inter-County Committee (SICC), which as the title indicates involved only counties, was established in the Detroit region in 1954; this council was superseded by the Southeast Michigan Council of Governments (SEMCOG), a more inclusive council involving municipalities and special districts as well as counties, in 1968. Since 1954 councils have been organized in all regions of the United States. A few of the early salient councils of governments organized and their date of establishment include: The Metropolitan Washington Council of Governments (Washington, D.C., 1957); Puget Sound Governmental

Conference (Seattle-Tacoma, 1957); Mid-Willamette Valley Council of Governments (Salem, Oregon, 1958); Association of Bay Area Governments (San Francisco, 1961); Southern California Association of Governments (Los Angeles, 1965); North Central Texas Council of Governments (Dallas-Fort Worth, 1966); Capitol Region Council of Elected Officials (Hartford, 1966);[2] East-West Gateway Coordinating Council (St. Louis, 1966); and, the Miami Valley Council of Governments (Dayton, Ohio, 1968). By 1966, according to one tabulation, there were forty-nine councils organized, with an additional seventy-seven under consideration or in the process of formation.[3] The following year, reflective of the growing number of councils, a national conference on councils and regionalism was conducted in Washington, D.C. At this time the National League of Cities and the National Association of Counties jointly established the National Service to Regional Councils, which later became known as the National Association of Regional Councils. This organization was created to provide assistance to locally elected officials involved in establishing councils. Three years later, that is by 1970, the number of established councils increased to 223.[4] According to the latest count, there are about 450 councils of governments functioning in the United States.[5] Included in the latter figure are some councils which have evolved from economic development districts and regional planning commissions.

## Local Support of Councils

What reasons account for the rapid proliferation of councils of governments over the past twenty years? Certainly there is no single answer to this query. To be sure, peculiar and local factors are partly responsible for the establishment of any one council of governments. Nevertheless, one basic reason for the proliferation of councils is that there appears to be, partially accounted for by the general failure of metropolitan governmental reform efforts, an "emerging consensus on the part of civic leaders and local officials . . . that the existing framework of local government is to be accepted essentially in its present form and that needed changes are to be sought within it through cooperative action."[6] The council-of-governments approach provides a politically feasible alternative for stimulating metropolitan consultation and collective regional action within the existing political framework.

Substantial empirical evidence is available to support the assertion that elected officials and other components of the local political elite, mindful of common and regional problems and the need for collective and cooperative action to confront these problems, view with favor the establishment of a council of governments in their region. To gain a clearer insight into the attitudes of selected actors involved in the local political process toward the council-of-governments mechanism, the author, in 1966 and 1967, carried out extensive field-survey research in Connecticut.[7] Semistructured in-depth interviews were conducted with the principal elected officials, city and town managers, and Democratic and Republican party chairmen in the three broadly defined regions of Hartford, New Haven, and Norwich-New London. The elected-official category included 47 mayors and first selectmen, the second category was comprised of 14 city and town managers, and the third group was composed of 112 political party chairmen, equally divided in party affiliation.[8]

The survey research found an impressive amount of support for the council-of-governments device in the Hartford, New Haven, and Norwich-New London regions. As can be seen from a cursory glance of the aggregate data presented in Table 1, seventy-four percent of those interviewed supported the formation of a typical council of governments in their area; that is, a council of an advisory capacity with a limited budget and staff. The prime purpose of such a council is, or would be, "to develop a consensus (among elected public officials from most or all of the governments of the region) regarding metropolitan needs and actions to be taken in solving . . . problems."[9]

TABLE 1

SUPPORT AND NONSUPPORT FOR REGIONAL COUNCIL

| CATEGORY | NUMBER (N=147) | APPROXIMATE PERCENT OF TOTAL |
|---|---|---|
| Favor advisory council | 108 | 74 |
| Favor council with powers | 16 | 11 |
| No need for any type of council | 18 | 12 |
| Favor "metropolitan government" | 5 | 3 |

As indicated by Table 1, approximately eleven percent of those interviewed favored the establishment of a council in their area that would be more than purely advisory; i.e., they supported a council with substantive powers and functions.[10] About twelve percent of the sample perceived no need for a council of elected officials in their area. Three percent, although amenable to the creation of a council in their area, suggested that a council was of doubtful value and revealed a preference for consolidated metropolitan or regional government.

As indicated by Table 2, where the data is presented on a regional basis, there is broad support for the council device in each of the three regions. In the Hartford area only one individual out of a total of seventy-four interviewed voiced dissent from the general consensus that there is a need for a council of governments. Almost three-fourths of the sample in the New Haven region agreed it would be desirable to establish a council in their area.

TABLE 2

SUPPORT AND NONSUPPORT FOR REGIONAL COUNCIL,
BY REGION

| CATEGORY | REGION (N=147) | | |
|---|---|---|---|
| | HARTFORD (N=74) | NEW HAVEN (N=40) | NORWICH-NEW LONDON (N=33) |
| Favor advisory council | 56 (76%) | 29 (73%) | 23 (70%) |
| Favor council with powers | 16 (22%) | 0 | 0 |
| No need for any type of council | 1 (1%) | 7 (17%) | 10 (30%) |
| Favor "metropolitan government" | 1 (1%) | 4 (10%) | 0 |

Somewhat more resistance to the council device was found in the Norwich-New London region. Only seventy percent of those interviewed in this area felt there was any need to establish a council. Moreover, respondents in this region supplied more than half (ten out of eighteen individuals) of those who were opposed to the council concept, yet the number of those interviewed in this region accounted for only about twenty-three percent of the total sample.

Greater opposition to the council-of-governments device manifested by the Norwich-New London sample is somewhat due to the largely rural and small-town character of the area and its less cohesive regional pattern.

A segmented analysis of the survey data allows us to examine in particular the attitude of the various components of the sample toward the council of governments device. As Table 3 suggests, there is generally widespread support among elected officials for the council device; conversely, no elected official identified himself with the notion of "metropolitan government." Not a single elected official in the Hartford area voiced a negative attitude toward the council concept. In the New Haven region, two Democratic and two Republican local officeholders saw no need to organize a council of governments in their area. Somewhat more resistance to the council device was manifested by local elected officials in the Norwich-New London region. Although the vast majority of the Republican elected officials interviewed placed themselves in favor of the council concept, three of the four Democratic elected officials were of the persuasion that a council of governments was not needed nor desired in their area.

As Table 4 illustrates, the vast majority of Democratic and Republican party chairmen interviewed were of the persuasion that a council of governments would be a desirable institution in their region; one is impressed with the substantial support that Democratic and Republican party chairmen give to the council device. As the data indicates, the type of council they generally favor is one of a typical nature. Only six party chairmen interviewed (three Democrats and three Republicans) favored providing the council any substantive powers and/or functions. It is of note that five Democratic party chairmen favored "metropolitan government." No Republican was identified with this position.

## TABLE 3

### Support and Nonsupport for Regional Council: Elected Officials by Party and Region

| CATEGORY | AREA (N=44) | | | | | |
| --- | --- | --- | --- | --- | --- | --- |
| | HARTFORD (N=18) | | NEW HAVEN (N=15) | | NORWICH-NEW LONDON (N=11) | |
| | DEM. (N=9) | REP. (N=9) | DEM. (N=5) | REP. (N=10) | DEM. (N=4) | REP. (N=7) |
| Favor advisory council | 8 (89%) | 9 (100%) | 3 (60%) | 8 (80%) | 1 (25%) | 5 (71%) |
| Favor council with added powers | 1 (11%) | 0 | 0 | 0 | 0 | 0 |
| No need for any council | 0 | 0 | 2 (40%) | 2 (20%) | 3 (75%) | 2 (29%) |
| Favor "metropolitan government" | 0 | 0 | 0 | 0 | 0 | 0 |

# TABLE 4

## SUPPORT AND NONSUPPORT FOR REGIONAL COUNCIL: DEMOCRATIC AND REPUBLICAN PARTY CHAIRMEN BY AREA

| CATEGORY | AREA (N=89) | | | | | |
|---|---|---|---|---|---|---|
| | HARTFORD (N=45) | | NEW HAVEN (N=24) | | NORWICH-NEW LONDON (N=20) | |
| | DEM. (N=19) | REP. (N=26) | DEM. (N=11) | REP. (N=13) | DEM. (N=7) | REP. (N=13) |
| Favor advisory council | 15 (79%) | 22 (85%) | 7 (64%) | 10 (76%) | 5 (71%) | 10 (76%) |
| Favor council with added powers | 3 (16%) | 3 (12%) | 0 | 0 | 0 | 0 |
| No need for any council | 0 | 1 ( 3%) | 0 | 3 (24%) | 2 (29%) | 3 (24%) |
| Favor "metropolitan government" | 1 ( 5%) | 0 | 4 (36%) | 0 | 0 | 0 |

Of the forty-five chairmen conversed with in the Hartford region, where, as previously noted, a council of governments has been organized,[11] only one party chairman, a Republican, voiced the opinion that a council was not desirable in the area. Three Democratic party chairmen believed that the council should have some powers; an equal number of Republican party chairmen agreed with this position. Although no Republican party chairmen interviewed supported "metropolitan government," one Democratic party chairman was so inclined.

As Table 4 indicates, no Democratic party chairmen in the New Haven area were opposed to organizing a council of governments in that region; three Republicans were. What is most surprising is that four Democratic party chairmen supported "metropolitan government." In neither of the two other regions, Hartford and Norwich-New London, did this author uncover as much support for "metropolitan government" among Democratic and Republican party leaders.

Stronger opposition to the council concept by Democratic and Republican party chairmen was found in the Norwich-New London region. One-quarter of the total party chairmen in this region registered their disbelief of the council concept. Further, not one party chairman believed that if a council were organized it should be invested with any powers. And all party chairmen, Republican and Democratic alike, looked askance at the notion of "metropolitan government."

A few general comments can be advanced relative to the attitude of Democratic and Republican party chairmen toward the council device. None of the party chairmen with whom this author conversed with believe that the council is, or would prove to be, a partisan issue. Secondly, it appears that party chairmen hold their beliefs about the council concept with less intensity than elected officials or town and city managers. One reason for this finding is that relatively few of the party chairmen are well aware of the concept of a regional council of locally elected officials. In addition, one suspects that party chairmen are less aware than practitioners of local government of the needs of their locality that perhaps could be better met through some sort of regional or semiregional cooperation.

The author interviewed twelve city and town managers in the Hartford area and three city and town managers in the Norwich-New London region.[12] (No manager forms of local government are currently in existence in the New Haven area.) Of the three categories of individuals interviewed, town and city managers are the most ardent supporters of the council device; no manager voiced opposition to the establishment of a council of governments in his area. Indeed eight of the managers in the Hartford region believe that the council should have substantive powers, although none of the three city or town managers in the Norwich-New London region shared this attitude. One suspects that their strong support for the council concept is a result of their education and work experience, as well as the demands of their profession. Curiously enough, none of the managers identified himself with the notion of "metropolitan government."

In summary, then, the Connecticut survey data indicates the council device gains broad support from locally elected officials, city and town managers, and party chairmen, at least in the three regions where the interviews were conducted. From the perspective of the respondents, the council device provides a useful forum for discussing and hopefully developing a collective response to mutual and regional problems. Support for formation of councils of governments is to some oblique degree accounted for by the success of municipal intergovernmental cooperation; many respondents feel that a council might well engender further local intergovernmental cooperation that would be of advantage and benefit to their community.[13]

There is additional data that may be cited indicating that locally elected officials favor the establishment of council bodies believing that such organizations can be effective in helping communities confront common and regional problems. In 1972, the Advisory Commission on Intergovernmental Relations (ACIR) and the International City Management Association (ICMA) sent a questionnaire to all city and county elected officials in jurisdictions with at least 5,000 population asking them: (1) why was a council formed in their area?; and (2) why did their government join the council? The survey found that city and county officials alike maintained the prime reason for the *formation* of a council in their area was due to the belief that such a body could further "initiate cooperative approaches to solving general regional problems."[14] Further, the ACIR and ICMA survey documented that two of the basic reasons local governments *join* councils are that local officials are persuaded that: (1) a council can serve as a "forum for discussion of regional problems"; and (2) it can "contribute significantly to the solution of local problems."[15]

Further empirical data relating to local support for councils of governments and central-city participation in these bodies is found in the study of Charles Harris entitled, *Regional COG's and the Central City*, published by the Metropolitan Fund of Detroit in 1970. Responding to a largely structured mail questionnaire, core-city mayors indicated the prime reason responsible for their locality joining the area regional council was out of the belief that such a council could provide, in the area, a "forum of discussion for regional problems."[16] Harris notes the second most important reason responsible for central-city participation in councils was due to the belief that these organizations "would improve cooperation between the central city and suburbs."[17] In addition, Harris found that a large proportion of the mayors responding to his survey were of the opinion that a council of governments established in their area could significantly contribute to the solution of core-city problems.[18]

In conclusion, from the perspective of local officials, a council of governments is an attractive institution for it provides a forum where mayors can converse about common and mutual problems and allows them to shape regional policies *relatively* free from external political interference. As one local official, long active in the Metropolitan Washington Council of Governments, has asserted:

> If we move to solve problems through the mutual cooperation approach of regional councils, local elected officials will retain control over regional matters. If we fail to deliver solutions, then our power to deal with the regional challenges will be moved to another level of government.[19]

Further, as Henry Schmandt has noted, the council device is politically acceptable because: (1) it leaves the existing pattern of local government undisturbed; (2) it provides for no major transfer of power from the local units to a larger agency; and (3) it is based on voluntary cooperation.[20] In addition, the council device is not viewed by most local officials as a transitory step toward "metropolitan government"; a development that most local, especially suburban, officials oppose.[21]

With reference to the Connecticut survey data cited earlier, as Table 5 documents, those respondents who reacted favorably to the establishment of a council of governments in their area assumed this stance partly out of the belief that such a council would not lead to the establishment of some version of "metropolitan government." Conversely, a majority of those opposed to the formation

**TABLE 5**

**COUNCIL DEVICE AND METROPOLITAN GOVERNMENT**

| CATEGORY | REGION (N=142) | | |
| --- | --- | --- | --- |
| | HARTFORD | NEW HAVEN | NORWICH-NEW LONDON |
| Among those who favor council | (N=72) | (N=29) | (N=23) |
| Step toward "metropolitan government" | | | |
| Yes | 21 (29%) | 2 (7%) | 4 (17%) |
| No | 51 (71%) | 27 (93%) | 19 (83%) |
| Among those against council | (N=1) | (N=7)[a] | (N=10) |
| Step toward "metropolitan government" | | | |
| Yes | 1 (100%) | 4 (67%) | 9 (90%) |
| No | 0 | 2 (33%) | 1 (10%) |

[a] Insufficient information to classify one respondent as believing whether council will lead to "metropolitan government"

of a council in their region, (albeit a distinct minority of the total sample), reacted negatively partially because they fear that such a council would be the first small step toward "metropolitan government."

Since local governmental membership and participation in councils is not subject to electorate ratification and because most councils have functioned without much saliency, little is known about mass citizen attitudes toward councils. Given the low profile of councils it is reasonable to assume that most of the populace is ignorant of councils of governments. However, some singular evidence does indicate a measure of popular support for councils. David R. Morgan, in his essay, "Attitudes Among Local Officials Toward a Council of Governments: The Oklahoma City Situation," notes that in the period 1967-68, the voters of three communities, whose governments are members of the Association of Central Oklahoma Governments (ACOG), in an advisory referendum upheld the participation of their local officials in the council by favorable margins ranging from fifty-six to sixty-seven percent.[22]

## The Federal Role

Notwithstanding the strong support for councils of governments at the local and regional level, one should note that Federal legislation and support, especially from the Department of Housing and Urban Development, has been quite instrumental in the proliferation and maintenance of councils. Indeed, some would assert that while local enthusiasm and support was primarily responsible for the formation of councils up to 1965, since that date the *most* important reason accounting for the establishment of councils has been federal encouragement and monetary support. Further, some observers of the urban scene maintain that without federal grant assistance the absolute number of councils would markedly decline.

As long ago as 1961 components of the federal government began promoting the council-of-governments concept. In that year, the Advisory Commission on Intergovernmental Relations (ACIR) went on record opposing the creation of additional metropolitan planning commissions, the governmental members of which are usually represented by *appointed* individuals. Instead, it opted for a council-of-governments organizationallike structure that would include as *ex officio* members mayors, councilmen, and county commissioners. In justifying this alternative, the ACIR asserted the desirability and need for integrating regional planning with decision making. In the same year, the Commission urged the several states to enact a model interlocal cooperation act that had been prepared in 1957 by the Committee of State Officials on Suggested Legislation of the Council of State Governments.[23] In 1962, the ACIR issued a report recommending that the establishment of metropolitan councils of governments be encouraged by the states. The Commission urged states to aid the formation of councils "by enacting the suggested legislation authorizing the making of interlocal agreements, supplemented by whatever special provisions may be required in the particular instance in according legal entity status to voluntary councils desirous of such status."[24]

As illustrated by Chart 1, legislation passed by Congress and implemented by the federal government during the period 1954-1971 encouraged the formation of councils of governments; in particular, legislation acted upon favorably by Congress in the sixties was of crucial importance. The Federal-Aid Highway Act of 1962 mandated a *regional* approach for highway planning. The Housing and Urban Development Act of 1965, which amended the Housing Act of 1954, provides federal funding for councils. Section 204 of the Demonstration Cities and Metropolitan Act of 1966 gives designated councils of governments the authority to review local applications for federal assistance for a wide variety of programs.

Section 701(g) of the Housing Act of 1965 allows the Department of Housing and Urban Development to make grants to regional councils covering two-thirds of the cost of studies, the collection of data, and the preparation of

## CHART 1
## ANNUAL GROWTH RATES OF REGIONAL COUNCILS, BY FEDERAL PROGRAM ENACTMENTS 1954-1971[a]

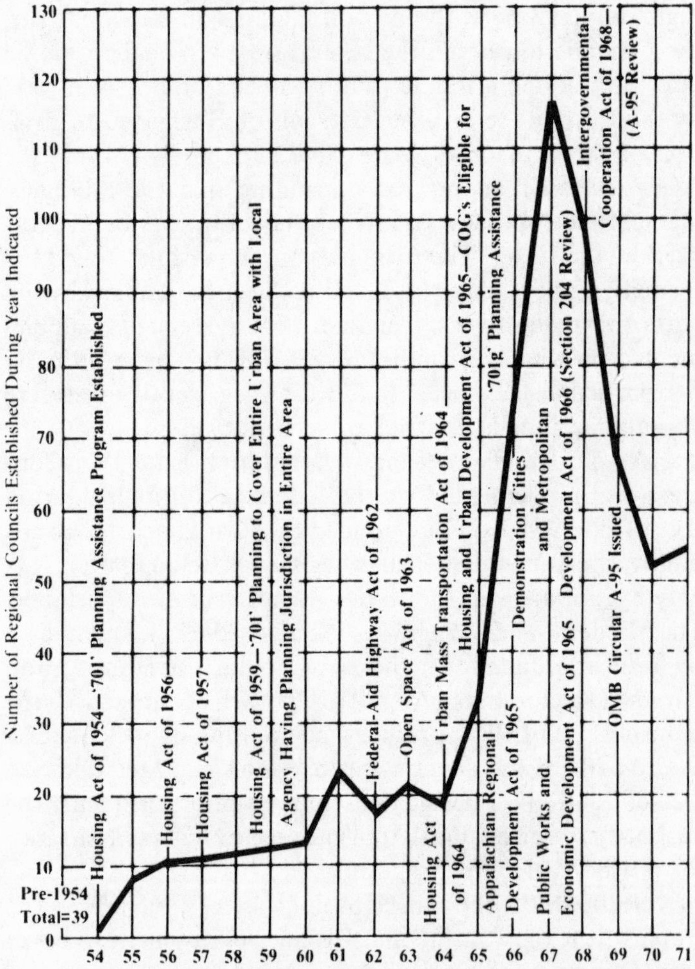


[a]*Source:* Advisory Commission on Intergovernment Relations, *Regional Decision Making: New Strategies for Sub-State Districts* (Washington, D.C.: The Commission, 1973), 76.

regional plans and programs. Relative to these grants the Urban Renewal Administration noted:

> The main objective of these grants is to foster metropolitan cooperation on a broad front by establishing and maintaining organizations of policy and decision-makers representing the various local governments within metropolitan areas. Such organizations are viewed as effective forums for studying and resolving issues raised by metropolitan problems, for the preparation of metropolitan comprehensive plans, for developing action programs for carrying out metropolitan comprehensive plans, and for determining regional policies affecting governmental and functional activities.[25]

A recent study issued by the Advisory Commission on Intergovernmental Relations noted that slightly more than two-fifths of all federal monies granted to councils in fiscal year 1971 was provided for under the terms of the above legislation.[26] The practical effect of this legislation was to expand the staff and programmatic activities of the existing councils and spur the establishment of additional councils.

Section 204 of the Demonstration Cities and Metropolitan Development Act of 1966 has proven to be of central importance in the proliferation of the council device. This act required, as of July 1, 1967, that all local governmental requests for federal assistance involving approximately forty grant and loan programs be initially reviewed by the appropriate designated regional review agency. Projects involved include airports, highways, hospitals, libraries, open-space land projects, sewerage facilities and waste-treatment plants, transportation facilities, water-development and land-conservation projects, and water-supply-and-distribution facilities. The purpose of this review is to ensure that all program applications are mindful and consistent with the regional needs of the area. As a result of this legislation, many new councils were formed and a large number of councils were designated by

41

the Department of Housing and Urban Development as the official review agency of their area. The Advisory Commission on Intergovernmental Relations found in 1972 that the *most important* reason for local governments joining councils related to the review requirements enunciated above.[27]

The Intergovernmental Cooperation Act of 1968, portions of which were implemented by Circular A-95, dated July 24, 1969, issued by the then Bureau of the Budget, now the Office of Management and Budget, expanded the regional review function of designated councils to include over 150 federally assisted programs. Specifically, the purposes of this review, as noted by Circular A-95, are twofold: (1) to assure better coordination of federally assisted projects, and (2) to stimulate intergovernmental cooperation in planning and development activities. As of 1973, 390 regional councils were designated as A-95 "Clearinghouses."[28]

Additional Federal support for regional councils is provided for by the Federal Water Pollution Control Act Amendment of 1972 and the Coastal Zone Management Act passed by Congress in the same year. Councils designated as review agencies are eligible for inclusion in coastal states' management programs for land and water resources under the Coastal Zone Management Act. The Rural Development Act, also passed by Congress in 1972, gives additional review responsibilities for nonmetropolitan councils.[29]

## The Role of the States

Although not to the marked degree of importance as the federal government, state support and executive and legislative policies have played an important role in the establishment of councils of governments.[30] In several instances, the state itself is a member of the regional council.

The state of Oregon is a member of the Mid-Willamette Valley Council of Governments, organized in 1958, located in the Salem, Oregon region. The East-West Gateway Coordinating Council in the St. Louis area has four state officials as nonvoting members, two from Illinois and a like number from Missouri. The legal basis of a majority of regional councils is derived from either a regional-planning-agency act or specific council-of-governments legislation. Approximately eleven percent of the councils derive their legal standing from legislation authorizing horizontal intergovernmental cooperation or the joint exercise of powers.[31] Hence, at minimum, all states provide directly or indirectly the necessary legal framework for the establishment and operation of councils of governments.

Various states provide financial as well as other forms of support for councils. A survey conducted in 1972 found that twenty states provided general support funds to councils and other regional planning organizations; in that year, states allocating at least $200,000 or more to regional councils included Arkansas, Connecticut, Georgia, Illinois, Kentucky, Michigan, Oklahoma, Texas, Vermont, Virginia, and Wisconsin. The average amount of state general support for each council was between $5,000 and $30,000.[32] In addition, some states, such as Pennsylvania, encourage the formation of COGs by providing manpower and technical assistance to local government officials interested in organizing such bodies.[33]

In some states, the rise of councils of governments constituted in part a reaction against perceived threatening state policy. In several states, legislation under consideration in the area of regional planning, deemed injurious to "home rule," engendered council-formation efforts. This was particularly true in California. There is substantial evidence to assert that the establishment of the Association of Bay Area Governments (ABAG), formed in the San

Francisco region in 1961, and the Southern California Association of Governments (SCAG), organized in the Los Angeles area in 1965, were initially viewed by many as "defensive" associations to be employed against threatening state policy. Regarding this point, Peter Douglas notes, with particular reference to the Southern California Association of Governments:

> Federal policy regarding intergovernmental relations in metropolitan areas and Federal pressures undoubtedly influenced local governments to form SCAG, but the influence of the Federal government was not decisive. The state Regional Planning Law of 1963, and specifically its escape clause was the primary stimulant, as indicated by numerous statements made during the planning and development of SCAG.[34]

In several states, the governor played an especially strong role in council-formation efforts. Former Governor Romney of Michigan was an early enthusiastic supporter of the council device. Romney asserted that rather than weakening local government, councils served to enhance their stature:

> They provide a forum for the interchange of information; they provide technical assistance to member governments and stimulate interlocal cooperation; [and] they provide a bridge between public officials and private citizens interested in enriching the urban environment.[35]

Likewise, former Governor John B. Connally of Texas was a strong supporter of the council device in his state. Phillip Barnes, writing about council developments in that state, noted:

> Early in 1966, then Governor John B. Connally lent the prestige and influence of his office to the regional council movement. Representatives from the Governor's office called upon local officials, offering advice and consultation in the formation of regional organizations; assumed the role of liaison between local officials and various federal agencies; and a state grant-in-aid program for the support of

COG activities was initiated. Since his election in 1968, Governor Preston Smith has strengthened this role by increased state funding and the promotion of long-range goals.[36]

## Summary and Conclusions

We can conclude that the establishment and rapid proliferation of councils of governments was due to both local and extraregional political factors. On the one hand, most locally elected officials believe there is a need for some sort of area-wide structure that can serve as a discussion forum for common local and regional problems, facilitate regional planning, and promote horizontal inter-governmental cooperation. The council of governments device best meets this need for it does not distort or threaten existing political institutions and arrangements; and, at the same time, it serves to enhance the position of local governments in the regional political complex.

Again, we should note that external political factors were also instrumental in the establishment of councils. Indeed, the increasing number of councils established since 1965 is directly related to federal legislation and support for councils. Certainly, it would be fair to suggest that the number of councils would be far fewer if the federal "carrot and stick" were absent. And as noted, states and state policy played their part in encouraging the formation of councils of governments, although the amount of state support varied considerably. In some states, such as Washington, Illinois, Oregon, Florida, and Texas, the state assumed almost a missionary posture promoting the COG concept, while in others, state encouragement and support of council-formation efforts were only of a minimal variety. General council dependence upon federal and state support is well reflected in the results of a recent survey that revealed that the directors of councils felt it was of utmost importance for them to maintain good council relationships with the federal and their respective state governments.[37]

# Notes

1. As an example, Robert H. Connery and Richard H. Leach stated in February 1964: ". . . although one of the paths to better metropolitan government taken with increasing frequency in recent years in non-southern areas—New York, Detroit, San Francisco, to name only three—has been the voluntary association of the existing governmental units in a regional council, only one such council has been created in the South—the Washington Metropolitan Council [sic] which has had very limited success—and *no others seem to be in the process of formation* (italics mine)." Yet within a very short time after this was written a number of councils of elected officials were functioning in the South. See Robert H. Connery and Richard H. Leach, "Southern Metropolis: Challenge to Government," *Journal of Politics* 26 (February 1964): 76.

2. Merged with the Capitol Region Planning Agency, 1974.

3. Metropolitan Washington Council of Governments, *Councils of Governments* (Washington, D.C.: The Council, 1966).

4. National Service to Regional Councils, *Regionalism: A New Dimension in Local Government and Inter-governmental Relations* (Washington, D.C.: The Service, 1971), p. 6.

5. Interview with Ralph Webster of the National Association of Regional Councils, June 20, 1974.

6. Henry J. Schmandt, "The Emerging Strategy," *National Civic Review* 55 (June 1966): 327.

7. Although the field research was conducted some years ago the author is of the opinion that the attitudinal response findings presented would be essentially similar if this research was replicated at the present time.

8. For the purposes of this study the author sought interviews with three individuals in sixty-one Connecticut communities located either in the Hartford, New Haven, or Norwich-New London regions. Generally, in each of the localities interviews were sought with the chief elected public official, i.e., mayor

or first selectman, as well as the Democratic and Republican party chairmen. However, in those communities where a manager form of government is employed, the author sought an interview with the manager instead of the chief elected public official. The interviews conducted were of a semistructured variety, and each averaged about an hour although many were of a much longer duration. A total of 183 interviews were sought; of this number, 146 were completed—approximately eighty percent. A segmental analysis of this latter figure is provided in the table below.

INTERVIEWS SOUGHT AND COMPLETED BY CATEGORY
OF INDIVIDUALS INTERVIEWED

| CATEGORY | INTERVIEWS SOUGHT | INTERVIEWS COMPLETED | PERCENTAGE OF INTERVIEWS COMPLETED |
|---|---|---|---|
| Elected Officials | | | |
| Democratic | 21 | 17 | 80 |
| Republican | 26 | 26 | 100 |
| Managers | 14 | 14 | 100 |
| Party Chairmen | | | |
| Democratic | 61 | 37 | 61 |
| Republican | 61 | 52 | 85 |

9. Norman Beckman, "Alternative Approaches for Metropolitan Reorganization," *Public Management* 46 (June 1964): 130.
10. By comparison, we should note that survey research conducted in the San Francisco Bay Area indicated that as many as thirty-five percent of the local officials interviewed favored transforming the Association of Bay Area Governments (ABAG) into a limited metropolitan government with various functional responsibilities. See Thomas E. Cronin,

"Metropolity Models and City Hall," *American Institute of Planners Journal* 36 (May 1970): 193.

11. Merged with Capitol Region Planning Agency, 1974.

12. One was serving as an acting manager.

13. For a further analysis of the Connecticut survey research findings, see by the author, "Attitudes Toward COGs in Connecticut," *Midwest Review of Public Administration* 5 (February 1971): 42-44, and also by the author, "Attitudes of Selected Political Actors in Connecticut Toward the Council of Governments Concept" mimeographed (Paper presented to the Maine Conference of Social Scientists, University of Maine, Orono, Maine, April 9, 1970).

14. Advisory Commission on Intergovernmental Relations, *Regional Decision Making: New Strategies for Substate Districts* (Washington, D.C.: The Commission, 1973), p. 117.

15. Ibid., p. 118.

16. Charles Harris, *Regional COG's and the Central City* (Detroit: Metropolitan Fund, 1970), p. 14.

17. Ibid.

18. Ibid.

19. Francis B. Francois, "Who Shall Make Our Regional Decisions?" *Nation's Cities* 10 (November 1972): 15.

20. Henry J. Schmandt, "The Area Council-Approach to Metropolitan Government," *Public Management* 42 (February 1960): 31.

21. Amos H. Hawley and Basil G. Zimmer, *The Metropolitan Community: Its People and Government* (Beverly Hills, Calif.: Sage Publications, 1970), p. 139.

22. David R. Morgan, "Attitudes Among Local Officials Toward a Council of Governments: The Oklahoma City Situation," *Midwest Review of Public Administration* 5 (February 1971): 37.

23. Joseph F. Zimmerman, "Metropolitan Ecumenism: The Road to the Promised Land?" *Journal of Urban Law* 44 (Spring 1967): 445.

24. Ibid.

25. Ibid., p. 442.

26. Advisory Commission on Intergovernmental Relations, *Regional Decision-Making,* p. 90.

27. Ibid., p. 118.

28. National Association of Regional Councils, *Regional Council Directory* (Washington, D.C.: The Association, 1973), p. v.

29. Jean Gansel, "Regional Council Directors: Perspectives of External Influence," in *The Municipal Yearbook, 1974* (Washington, D.C.: International City Management Association, 1974), p. 52.

30. For a good review of the several states' role in promoting councils of governments and regionalism in general, see Richard C. Hartman, "The State's Role in Regionalism," in *The Regionalist Papers,* ed. Kent Mathewson (Detroit: Metropolitan Fund, 1974), pp. 236-253.

31. Advisory Commission on Intergovernmental Relations, *Regional Decision Making,* p. 79.

32. Hartman, "The State's Role in Regionalism," p. 250.

33. William C. Seyler, "Interlocal Relations: Cooperation," *The Annals of the American Academy of Political and Social Science* 416 (November 1974): 163-164.

34. Peter Douglas, *The Southern California Association of Governments: A Response to Federal Concern for Metropolitan Areas* (Los Angeles: Institute of Government and Public Affairs, University of California, 1968), p. 22.

35. George Romney, "Special Message on Local Affairs" mimeographed (Transmitted to the 74th Michigan Legislature, East Lansing, Michigan, March 31, 1967), p. 5.

36. Philip W. Barnes, "Experience in Texas," *Midwest Review of Public Administration* 5 (February 1971): 41.

37. Gansel, "Regional Council Directors," p. 52.

# The Formation
and Attributes
of Councils
of Governments

# 3

As the preceding discussion demonstrated, the rise and proliferation of councils of governments is primarily due to two factors: On the one hand, there is a desire on the part of elected officials of metropolitan and nonmetropolitan regions to create a permanent forum structure where like elected public officials can convene on a periodic basis and discuss matters of common concern. As a corollary of this, public officials believe there is a need for the multiplicity of governments in their area to adopt a common and somewhat unified program of action to cope with a variety of problems. On the other hand, as has been elaborated upon, councils have been a manifest result of various federal and state policies and programs promoting regionalism on the local level.

## Formation Efforts
## on Behalf of Councils

However widespread locally elected officials entertain the desirability of establishing a council of governments in their area, the arduous task of forming such bodies has often been left to the efforts of a dedicated few; one cannot overemphasize this crucial assertion. Indeed, it is possible to identify those individuals who were primarily responsible for organizing each of the ten councils of governments that were central to this study. Table 6 provides this information.

TABLE 6

PRIME ORGANIZERS: COUNCILS OF GOVERNMENTS

| ABBREVIATED NAMES [a] | PRIME ORGANIZERS [b] |
|---|---|
| ABAG | Mayors of Pacifica, Berkeley, San Rafael, Livermore<br>City Manager of Berkeley<br>Supervisor of City-County of San Francisco |
| COG | President of the District Board of Commissioners, Washington, D.C.<br>Two State Senators (one from Virginia, the other from Maryland)<br>"Few others" |
| CRCEO | Employee of the Greater Hartford Chamber of Commerce<br>Suburban First Selectman |
| MACLOG | Commissioner of DeKalb County |
| M-WVCOG | City Administrator of Salem |
| PSGC | County Commissioners |
| RCEO | President of Penjerdel [c]<br>Commissioner of Montgomery County<br>Mayor of Philadelphia |
| SCAG | City Councilman of Burbank<br>Official of the League of California Cities (eventually became City Manager of Claremont)<br>"Five other city and county people" |

52

TABLE 6—*Continued*
SEMCOG    Three members of selected Policy Committee
established by Metropolitan Fund
Member of the Board of Commissioners of Oakland
County
Chairman, Metropolitan Fund
President, Metropolitan Fund
"Others"

SICC    Chairman of the Board of Supervisors of Wayne County
Chairman of the Board of Supervisors of Macomb
County
Chairman of the Board of Supervisors of Oakland County

---

[a]Key to abbreviated names: ABAG—Association of Bay Area Governments; COG—Metropolitan Washington Council of Governments; CRCEO—Capitol Region Council of Elected Officials; MACLOG—Metropolitan Atlanta Council of Local Governments; M-WVCOG—Mid-Willamette Valley Council of Governments; PSGC—Puget Sound Governmental Conference; RCEO—Regional Conference of Elected Officials; SCAG—Southern California Association of Governments; SEMCOG—Southeast Michigan Council of Governments; and SICC—Supervisors' Inter-County Committee.

[b]Various sources were utilized for discerning the prime organizers of the councils. With reference to ABAG, see Institute of Local Self Government, *ABAG, Appraised: A Quinquennial Review of Voluntary Regional Cooperative Action Through the Association of Bay Area Governments,* (2nd ed.; Berkeley, California: Institute for Local Self Government, 1967), pp. 8-14.

With reference to COG, see Royce Hanson, *The Politics of Metropolitan Cooperation: Metropolitan Washington Council of Governments* (Washington, D.C.: Washington Center for Metropolitan Studies, 1964), p. 1; Roscoe Martin, "The Conference Approach: The Metropolitan Washington Council of Governments," in *Metropolis in Transition* (Washington, D.C.: Government Printing Office, 1963), pp. 42-43; and Jack Eisen, "COG Adds Action to 10 Years of Talk," *The Washington Post,* 11 April 1967, p. B-1. Also verified by interview with Walter Scheiber, executive director of COG, June 8, 1967.

TABLE 6—*Continued*

With reference to CRCEO, see William N. Casella, Jr., "Regional Approach Stressed in Connecticut," *National Civic Review* 55 (April 1966): 212-213; and by the same author, "Town Meeting Held in Greater Hartford," *National Civic Review* 54 (January 1965): 36-38; and Rosaline Levenson, "Hartford Considers Regional Agencies," *National Civic Review* 55 (November 1966): 591-593. Also verified by interview with Walter Aston, chairman of CRCEO, August 10, 1967 and interview with Dana Hansen, Manager of Regional Development, Greater Hartford Chamber of Commerce, August 8, 1967.

With reference to MACLOG, see Jack Spaulding, "The Community Group Fills the Vacuum," *Atlanta Journal,* 18 September 1966, p. 28; and "Metro Officials Are Planning an Organization," *Georgia Municipal Journal* 14 (July 1964): 17. Also verified by interview with Glenn E. Bennett, secretary of MACLOG, June 13, 1967.

With reference to M-WVCOG see Martin, "The Conference Approach: The Mid-Willamette Valley Council of Governments," in *Metropolis in Transition,* p. 29-30; Richard Hartman, "Massive Cooperation—The Next Step?," *Western City* 35 (January 1959): 19. Also verified by interview with Kent Mathewson, president of the Metropolitan Fund, Detroit (formerly City Administrator of Salem, Oregon), June 15, 1967.

With reference to PSGC, see David D. Rowlands, "Governmental Cooperation Promotes Regional Planning," *Public Management* 42 (April 1960): 81.

With reference to RCEO, see John W. Bodine, "Local Government Cooperation—Solution to Metropolis," *Public Management* 43 (October 1961): 226; and *Philadelphia Bulletin,* 11 June 1961, 2, July 1961, and 19 January 1966. Also verified by interview with Chester A. Kunz, executive director of RCEO, June 6, 1967.

With reference to SCAG, see David L. Baker, "Case History of the Southern California Association of Governments," *Minutes of the AMANACO Workshop on Regional Cooperation* (Washington, D.C.: National Association of Counties, 1964), pp. 19-21; and David Mars, *The Formation of SCAG: A Case History* (Los Angeles: School of Public Administration, University of Southern California, 1966).

TABLE 6—*Continued*

With reference to SEMCOG, see Citizens Research Council of Michigan, "Southeast Michigan Regionalism," in *The Regionalist Papers,* ed. Kent Mathewson (Detroit: Metropolitan Fund, 1974), pp. 56-69. Also verified by telephone conversation with James Thomas, information service officer, SEMCOG, July 24, 1975.

With reference to SICC, see William R. Gable, "The Metropolitan Council as a Device to Foster and Coordinate Intergovernmental Cooperation," in *Regional Organization,* Part III (Detroit: Metropolitan Fund, 1965), p. 95; also verified by interview with Gerard H. Coleman, executive director of SICC, June 16, 1967.

cPenjerdel is a nonprofit organization that sponsors or conducts research on metropolitan problems in the greater Philadelphia area.

It is of note that the organization of the cited councils has been the product of a dedicated few. In the instance of six of the councils included in Table 6, single individuals are generally acknowledged as being almost singularly responsible for organizing each of five of the councils, and the sixth is the product of two individuals.[1] The Metropolitan Washington Council of Governments (COG) was largely the product of Robert E. McLaughlin, a former president of the District Board of Commissions of Washington, D.C.; Edward Connor, a former chairman of the Board of Supervisors of Wayne County, was the motivating force behind the formation of the Supervisors' Inter-County Committee (SICC), which was succeeded by the Southeast Michigan Council of Governments (SEMCOG) in 1968. Chester A. Kunz, a former executive director, as well as countless others, credits John W. Bodine (at the time, president of Penjerdel) with "practically organizing the Regional Council of Elected Officials of the Philadelphia area singlehandedly." Most acknowledge that Charlie Emmerich, a former commissioner of De

Kalb County, was the key individual involved in organizing the former Metropolitan Atlanta Council of Local Governments (MACLOG). Kent Mathewson, a one-time city administrator of Salem, Oregon, and now president of the Metropolitan Fund of Detroit, was primarily responsible for organizing the Mid-Willamette Valley Council of Governments (M-WVCOG). Two individuals, Dana Hansen, at the time an employee of the Greater Hartford Chamber of Commerce, and Walter Aston, a suburban officeholder, are generally credited for being primarily responsible for organizing the Capitol Region Council of Elected Officials in the Hartford, Connecticut area (CRCEO).[2] Hansen, queried why he devoted such a great deal of time and effort in organizing CRCEO stated:

> Well, we at the Chamber are interested in regional problems. All kinds of problems beset this area . . . from inadequate services to a tax structure which favors the suburbs and small towns and makes the core city poor. Perhaps the biggest problem, though, is that of race . . . of the Negroes. And then there is the problem of leadership. The real leaders of the region live in the suburbs . . . [they] have left Hartford or never lived there in the first place. We thought by setting up CRCEO we could better deal with these things.[3]

An examination of Table 6 reveals that the paradigm of council-formation leadership was decidedly uneven. Although personalities identified with the core city were largely responsible for organizing COG, SICC, W-MVCOG, and, to a limited extent, CRCEO, SEMCOG, and RCEO, central-city leadership had comparatively little to do with the establishment of MACLOG, ABAG, SCAG, and PSGC; rather, in the instance of the latter organizations, suburban leadership was largely responsible for organizing the council. Indeed, the core cities of San Francisco and Los Angeles maintained virtually no involvement with ABAG and SCAG respectively during their formative period.

Various organizations were instrumental in assisting in the establishment of a majority of the councils listed in Table 7; groups played a supporting organizing role in the case of eight of the ten councils. Organization support for

TABLE 7

ORGANIZATIONS INVOLVED IN INITIATING COUNCILS OF GOVERNMENTS[a]

| COUNCIL | ORGANIZATIONS INVOLVED |
|---------|------------------------|
| ABAG | League of California Cities<br>County Supervisors' Association |
| COG | None |
| CRCEO | Greater Hartford Chamber of Commerce<br>League of Women Voters |
| MACLOG | Atlanta Region Metropolitan Planning Commission |
| M-WVCOG | Chamber of Commerce |
| PSGC | Washington Municipal League<br>Puget Sound Regional Planning Council |
| RCEO | Penjerdel |
| SCAG | County Supervisors' Association<br>League of California Cities<br>Coordinating Council on Urban Policy[b] |
| SEMCOG | Metropolitan Fund<br>Citizens Research Council of Michigan<br>Committee of 100 |
| SICC | None |

[a]Information for Table 7 was derived from the same sources as employed to assemble data for Table 6; see footnote b, Table 6.

[b]At the time, the (California) Coordinating Council on Urban Policy was a state body charged with advising the

TABLE 7—*Continued*
> governor on matters relevant to metropolitan areas. Its members included city, county, and school-district officials.

the formation and establishment of councils was of a multifarious character. But in each instance, with the exception of CRCEO, M-WVCOG, and SEMCOG, groups involved in council formation activities and efforts are those of a "narrow" focus and orientation almost exclusively concerned with local and county governmental organization and activities. What is important to note is simply this: the establishment of councils engendered only a limited, if any, amount of group activity on behalf of formation efforts. Further, of equally crucial and significant importance, there were no group efforts mounted designed to forestall councils from coming into existence.

It is difficult to generalize about the importance and value of group assistance rendered on behalf of the formation of councils. In several instances, organization assistance seems to have been of crucial importance in the establishment of a council. The Regional Advisory Committee of the Greater Hartford Chamber of Commerce played an important role in the creation of CRCEO. As one observer notes:

> The individuals who got the Council underway were those of the Regional Advisory Committee. They visited the elected officials of the region . . . tried to sell them on CRCEO. Yes, they did the formative organization work. Oh, they had a little help from several women of the League of Women Voters. But for the most part, the Regional Advisory Committee people did most of the work.[4]

The Committee of 100, composed of leading academic, business, and governmental figures, established by the Metropolitan Fund, did much of the groundwork that led to the formation of the Southeast Michigan Council of Governments. In other instances, the extent and nature of assistance organizations rendered on behalf of council-formation efforts varied, but usually involved financial aid, materials, office space, and/or staff. In several cases, a local government or organization served as the initial secretariat of the council during its formative stage. Despite what appears to be the trivial character of this assistance, its importance should not be minimized. In retrospect, the most important contribution organizations extended to councils during their nascent period was that of "legitimizing," usually through sponsoring regional citizen forums and other means, the need to establish a council of governments, which in turn engendered further funding and manpower assistance on behalf of council formation.[5]

Some years ago, Royce Hanson, formerly of American University, penned that councils of governments are invariably organized in an environment of a low public consciousness; Hanson notes, ". . . Public knowledge of the councils [while being formed] is limited to the civic leaders and the media representatives specifically concerned with regional problems."[6] This appears to be substantially true. With reference to each of the councils cited, only a few individuals and organizations had any involvement with their formation and consequent establishment. This is simply because councils, being the essentially voluntary and advisory bodies they are, raise little apprehension and conflict in the larger metropolitan political complex.

One further important observation can be advanced relating to the formation of councils. Based on the materials assembled and interviews conducted by the author—when each of the councils was in the process of being organized—no partisan political activity was engendered either in support of or opposition to council-formation efforts. Democratic and Republican party leaders, *func-*

*tioning as party leaders*, remained for the most part favorably disposed but essentially passive toward the emergence of ABAG, SCAG, CRCEO, and the other council bodies. Declared one Democratic leader regarding the rise of the Capital Region Council of Elected Officials:

> Oh, yes, I think that the Council is a good thing. . . . No, it is not a partisan issue at all. The party people had nothing to do with organizing it . . . nor the elected officials. It was the Chamber [Regional Advisory Committee] people who put the thing together. . . . They did the work.[7]

The lack of a partisan political response to the rise of councils is primarily accounted for by the fact that councils are perceived by party leaders as bodies of a nonthreatening character, not disruptive of established power and voter alignments. Reflective of this view is the comment of one former leading California politician some years ago asserting that councils "do not amount to much."[8]

## Participation Patterns of
## Eligible Governmental Units

There proved to be an uneven pattern of initial participation of eligible governments in councils when they were first organized. Of the ten councils that served as the focus of this study, one may conveniently divide them into two categories with regard to the level and extent of initial participation of local governmental units: (1) those that enjoyed almost universal participation of eligible governmental bodies, but usually restricted the kind of jurisdiction that could partake in council membership; and, (2) those that pursued a rather nonrestrictive membership policy and attracted to their ranks a substantial percentage of eligible governmental units, but something less than universal participation. The former category is composed of PSGC, M-WVCOG, CRCEO, COG, and the former SICC; in the latter category is included ABAG, SCAG,

SEMCOG, and the former RCEO and MACLOG ill-fated council organizations.

Practically all councils of governments that achieved total or almost universal participation of eligible governments from the outset limited their eligible and potential membership; this accounts for their success in securing universal membership recruitment. For example, as the name implies, only counties in the Detroit area were members of SICC. Membership in PSGC was initially open only to counties; then in 1959 membership was made available to the major cities of the region. Whereupon, three of the four eligible cities joined PSGC that year, while the remaining city opted to affiliate in 1963. As a result of adopting more flexible membership rules, membership in PSGC eventually expanded to four counties, thirty-three cities and towns, and two Indian tribes![9] M-WVCOG was established pursuant to an agreement entered into by its five members: the City of Salem, two counties, a school district, and the State of Oregon; no attempt has been made by this council to enlarge its membership. Only major governments, that is, jurisdictions with populations of 10,000 or greater, may partake in the activities of COG. Of all the councils that were central to this study, CRCEO is the only council that did not restrict the character of its membership, and yet at the same time enjoyed practically universal membership participation from its inception.[10]

As indicated previously, ABAG, SCAG, SEMCOG, and the former RCEO and MACLOG each sought a more inclusive participation of local governments in their organizations than those councils that effectively limited membership. Yet, as Table 8 documents, a substantial number of eligible governments did opt for membership in ABAG, SCAG, RCEO, and MACLOG during their nascent period.

Several observations may be advanced concerning initial local governmental participation in the councils contained in Table 8. ABAG, SCAG, and MACLOG were much more successful than RCEO and SEMCOG in their

TABLE 8

INITIAL MEMBERS: COUNCILS OF GOVERNMENTS[a]

| COUNCIL | INITIAL MEMBERS |
| --- | --- |
| ABAG | Six of nine eligible counties<br>Fifty-four of eighty-four eligible cities/<br>towns |
| MACLOG | Five of six eligible counties<br>Twenty-one of forty-five eligible cities/<br>towns |
| RCEO | Six of eleven eligible counties<br>Thirty-one of three hundred seventy-<br>seven eligible cities/towns |
| SCAG | Five of six eligible counties<br>Eighty of one hundred forty-nine eligible<br>cities/towns |
| SEMCOG | Five of six eligible counties<br>About one hundred of approximately<br>four hundred eligible cities/towns and<br>special districts |

[a]Information for Table 8 was derived from the same sources as employed to assemble data for Table 6; see footnote b, Table 6.

initial recruitment efforts. And second, while several of the councils enjoyed early membership of the core city, the remainder did not. Philadelphia was an early active member of the ill-fated RCEO. Former Mayors Richardson Dilworth and James Tate were strong proponents of RCEO. Indeed, their pronounced efforts on behalf of RCEO proved to be, on occasion, a source of embarrassment to the organization. Atlanta was a founding member of MACLOG. In contrast, San Francisco did not join ABAG until 1964, three years after the birth of the council; and, both the city and county of Los Angeles were late joiners of SCAG. And finally, as will be expanded upon, each of the above councils were generally successful in augmenting their membership ranks after being in existence for some period of time.

Based on the materials gathered, it is difficult to discern any paradigm relating to the type of locality whose government desired to be a charter member of a council. For instance, in some councils the core city was an active and early member, while in other cases, the core city refrained from early council involvement. To some degree, the personal qualities of individual elected local officials and *whether or not they entertain somewhat of a regional perspective*[11] rather than a purely local orientation appears to have been crucial in whether any one governmental unit opted at an early date to join a council. Declared the former Executive Director of RCEO:

> No, I don't think that socioeconomic characteristics [of a governmental jurisdiction] have much to do with it [whether a locality joins the council]. . . . It's personalities that count. . . . You have to get to the personalities . . . to the elected officials with your appeal. If you can reach the elected officials of any one town . . . chances are it will join. . . . No, socioeconomic characteristics have little to do with it. . . . In RCEO we have Philadelphia and a multitude of small communities. You have to reach the personalities of a community. . . .[12]

Further, it seems clear that some elected suburban officials are initially reluctant to their locality joining a council simply because they perceive central city domination of the organization and further they feel, that by partaking in the activities of the council, their community will be drawn into the problems of the core city. For instance, one elected official, relating to the author why his community had not joined CRCEO, stated:

> Initially all of the citizens of this community favored joining CRCEO. But then the town had a hearing on it and a smart lawyer was influential in swinging probably a majority of the citizens away from the device, a majority of the citizens, that is, who know anything about what is going on. He told the people, that if they joined the council, Somers would get involved in the problems of Hartford. . . . No, it was not a partisan issue . . . both parties came out in favor of Somers' joining the Council. It was that lawyer who turned the tables.[13]

Negative feelings toward Hartford also were instrumental in accounting for another community not affiliating with CRCEO during its nascent period. Responding to why his locality had not sought membership in the Council, one town manager asserted:

> The councilmen of this town voted against Windsor joining CRCEO because they feel that Hartford is not doing enough to solve its own problems. They think, like many of the people who live here, that Hartford wants the suburbs to solve its problems. . . . Beyond that, most of the people in Windsor have a very negative attitude of the politics in Hartford . . . and they don't want to get tied into that.[14]

In a somewhat similar vein, the Republican town chairman stated: "No, we are not a member of the Council. Why should we get involved with the problems of Hartford? We don't want anything to do with Hartford. . . . That is why most of the people who live in our town moved from Hartford."[15]

After functioning for some period of time, councils of governments that maintain a rather nonrestrictive membership policy are generally successful in attracting additional members to their ranks. This development is accounted for by basically two reasons. First, local governmental officials, who were initially apprehensive about the organization, upon observing council activity and policies no longer perceive the body as a threat to the political autonomy of their community. And second, the early activities of councils, albeit often of a mundane and unspectacular quality, serve to enhance their legitimacy and worth in the area, thereby attracting additional members.

Reflective of the above, both ABAG and SCAG have generally increased their total membership since their inception. In its early years ABAG was especially successful in augmenting its membership ranks. Beginning with an initial membership of sixty (six counties and fifty-four cities and towns) in 1961, by November 1962 it had sixty-seven members (seven counties and sixty cities and towns).[16] As of December 1, 1965, eighty-six (eight counties and seventy-eight cities) local government units belonged to ABAG.[17] On December 1, 1974, eighty-five of the ninety-two cities and seven of the nine counties in the San Francisco area were participants in the activities of the council.[18] Total membership in SCAG has grown from sixty members (six of the nine eligible counties and eighty of the 149 cities) to 130 members, including all six eligible counties and 124 of the 150 eligible cities.[19] In contrast to the experience of ABAG and SCAG, the total number of members of SEMCOG has remained rather constant at about one hundred.[20]

The number of local governments belonging to each council of governments varies. Some councils have fewer than a half dozen members, while others have a membership in excess of one hundred. According to one study, the average number of members of a nonmetropolitan regional council is about twenty (four counties and sixteen municipalities), while an average of about thirty-nine local governments (five counties and thirty-five municipalities) partake in the activities of urban regional councils.[21]

One final observation should be noted regarding local

governmental participation in councils of governments. Once they have formally joined, few governments terminate their council membership, although a few instances may be cited of where members have withdrawn from councils. After being a member for about a year, Macomb County terminated its membership with SEMCOG in February, 1972. The withdrawal of Macomb County from SEMCOG was due to a variety of reasons but of crucial importance was that the Council became identified, fairly or unfairly, with busing for the purposes of racial integration in the public schools, which is opposed by a majority of citizens in Macomb County.[22] Sonoma County withdrew from ABAG in April, 1972.[23] In a dispute over representation, Oklahoma City terminated its membership with the Association of Central Oklahoma Governments (ACOG) in August, 1972, but rejoined the organization two months later.[24]

## Organizational
## Structure of Councils

The basic representational body of a council of governments is the general assembly. Each local governmental member is usually represented by its chief elected official. About half of the councils provide equal voting rights to their members in the general assembly, although eleven percent apportion votes according to the population of each member unit. Thirty-nine percent of the councils utilize some other kind of standard to determine the voting privileges of each member.[25] In addition to chief elected local officials, some councils provide membership in their general assembly for other public officials. For instance, the Metropolitan Washington Council of Governments (COG) includes in its general assembly all members of the Maryland and Virginia state legislatures elected from districts in the Washington Standard Metropolitan Statistical Area (SMSA), and all members of the United States Congress elected, in whole or in part, by the electorate of the metropolitan region. The East-West Gateway Coordinating Council of the St. Louis area includes four state officials in its assembly as nonvoting members: the chief engineer of the Illinois Division of Highways, the chief engineer of the Missouri State Highway Commission, the director of the Illinois Department of Business and Economic Development, and the director of the Missouri State Division of Commerce and Industrial Development.

The general membership of each council of governments usually convenes twice a year, although some council assemblies meet as often as six times a year, while other councils hold but a single meeting each year for the members of their general assembly.[26] At these gatherings, which are usually structured in terms of agenda content, the representatives either meeting in a body or in workshops discuss the various problems confronting the region. Also, they consider and act upon general policy recommendations brought before them by the council leadership and usually annually elect the officers of the organization.

Except in those instances where councils have a limited membership, the functions of specific policy-making and program development are vested in the body of the executive committee or board; further, most councils hold the executive committee ultimately responsible for the expenditure of funds. By design, the size of executive committees are relatively small in number; the average size of an executive committee is about eleven members, although some committees have as many as thirty-five; while others have as few as three members.[27] The members of the executive committee are usually elected by the delegates of the general assembly, although many council bylaws ensure representation on these bodies to a certain type or combination of members. Invariably, councils guarantee core cities representation on the executive committee. About half the councils provide members of the executive board with equal voting privileges, while eleven percent distribute voting strength on the basis of population. The remaining councils utilize some other standard for determining voting privileges on the executive committee.[28] The members of the executive committee usually meet once a month to transact council business. For the day-to-day operation of the council, the executive committee retains, in most cases, a full-time administrator who serves at their pleasure; in turn, the executive director hires supporting staff.

Councils establish various policy committees for setting priorities and developing work programs. These committees are composed primarily of representatives of the general assembly, although sometimes individuals with demonstrated expertise, who are not council representatives, are also appointed to these committees. The functional concerns of these bodies include, but are not limited to, such matters as (1) land use, (2) criminal justice, (3) human resources, and (4) transportation. In addition, some councils create advisory technical committees, often composed of a professional council staff, that provide the policy committees with technical advice.

A review of the basic organizational structure of the Southern California Association of Governments (SCAG) provides the reader with a good understanding of the nature of council organization.[29] As can be seen in Chart 2, the basic representational unit of SCAG is the general assembly, which is generally composed of one elected representative and a single alternate from each of the 124 cities and six counties that are members of the council. The City of Los Angeles, however, has three delegates and a like number of alternates in the general assembly. The members of the general assembly convene twice a year.

# CHART 2[a]
## ORGANIZATIONAL STRUCTURE OF THE
## SOUTHERN CALIFORNIA ASSOCIATION OF GOVERNMENTS

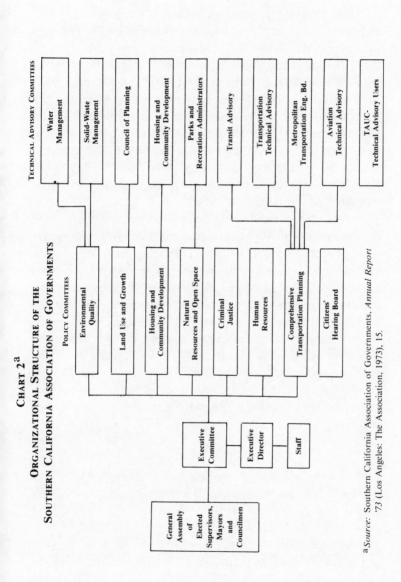

**TECHNICAL ADVISORY COMMITTEES**

- Water Management
- Solid-Waste Management
- Council of Planning
- Housing and Community Development
- Parks and Recreation Administrators
- Transit Advisory
- Transportation Technical Advisory
- Metropolitan Transportation Eng. Bd.
- Aviation Technical Advisory
- TAUC-Technical Advisory Users

**POLICY COMMITTEES**

- Environmental Quality
- Land Use and Growth
- Housing and Community Development
- Natural Resources and Open Space
- Criminal Justice
- Human Resources
- Comprehensive Transportation Planning
- Citizens' Hearing Board

- Executive Committee
- Executive Director
- Staff
- General Assembly of Elected Supervisors, Mayors and Councilmen

[a] *Source:* Southern California Association of Governments, *Annual Report '73* (Los Angeles: The Association, 1973), 15.

69

The leadership body of SCAG is the executive committee; it meets once a month and is composed of eighteen members. Members of the executive committee include three delegates and a similar number of alternates from the City of Los Angeles, one delegate and an alternate from each member county (chosen by the member cities in each county as their representative) and three at-large delegates and alternates, selected from the local jurisdictions by the committee. From within its ranks, the executive committee selects a president and vice president of SCAG. (The appointed executive director serves as the secretary-treasurer of the organization.)

Assisting the executive committee in the determination of SCAG policies are seven policy committees composed of local officials. The subject matter of these committees include: (1) land use and growth, (2) criminal justice, (3) environmental quality, (4) housing and community development, (5) human resources, (6) natural resources and open space, and (7) comprehensive transportation planning. Ten technical advisory committees, composed of SCAG professional staff, convey technical information and assistance on matters such as parks and recreation, housing and community development, transportation, and other regional matters to the policy committees.

## Council Staff

In reality, it is neither the general assembly nor the executive committee of the council, but rather the executive director and his staff who are *primarily* involved in program development and implementation. As Joseph Zimmerman has written, "The role of staff in quickly organizing the council and initiating projects cannot be minimized. Most council members lack the time required to initiate projects and conduct the necessary negotiations with local, state, and national officials."[30] During the mid-fifties and early sixties when councils of governments first made their appearance on the urban scene, council staff was generally limited. Most councils simply employed an executive director and a secretary. A few, such as the Puget Sound Governmental Conference (PSGC) retained the services of a professional planner. Given their limited staff, many councils relied on other public agencies for assistance. For instance, the Metropolitan Atlanta Council of Local Governments (MACLOG) often depended on the staff of the Atlanta Region Metropolitan Commission; indeed, the executive director of the Planning Commission was the secretary of MACLOG; and, he asserted at the time that it was difficult to determine where the duties of MACLOG ended and where the activities of the Planning Commission began.[31] The Supervisors' Inter-County Committee (SICC) utilized to a substantial degree the resources of the Detroit Metropolitan Area Regional Planning Commission. During its nascent period the Metropolitan Washington Council of Governments (COG) relied heavily on the District Government of Washington, D.C. for assorted aid; for some period of time the office of COG was located in the office building of the District Government.

In contrast to the earlier period, most councils of governments currently employ a considerable number of professional and supporting personnel. A study completed in 1972 found the mean number of employees retained by regional councils was fourteen, while those councils functioning in areas of 500,000 population or greater had a mean number of thirty-seven employees.[32] Of course, some councils employ a much larger number of employees than the mean. For instance, the Metropolitan Washington Council of Governments (COG) for the fiscal year 1975 had 175 authorized positions, of which 153 were filled.[33] The Southern California Association of Governments

(SCAG) employs approximately 100 professional and supporting employees.[34] The Association of Bay Area Governments (ABAG) has a work force of about seventy;[35] approximately an equal number of individuals are employed by the Puget Sound Governmental Conference (PSGC).[36]

A few comments concerning the backgrounds and responsibilities of council executive directors and professional staff personnel are appropriate here. About ninety-one percent of the executive directors are employed on a full-time basis.[37] The overwhelming majority of executive directors of councils of governments have been trained as planners, although a fair proportion have academic backgrounds in the social sciences. Most executive directors were affiliated with another regional council or served as a municipal or metropolitan planner before assuming their present position. A considerable number of executive directors previously served as city or county managers.[38] Generally, besides administering the council, executive directors are responsible for agenda formulation, project development, and budget development. They share the responsibilities of policy formation and citizen public relations with the members of the executive board.[39] Viewed in terms of roles, Laurie S. Frankel and Walter A. Scheiber have written: "They [executive directors] function as politicians, fund-raisers, grantsmen, program innovators and coordinators, policy initiators, and as administrators." And of especial import they add, "Regional council executives continually work toward maintaining the interest of elected officials in the regional process and toward seeking consensus among council members."[40] It need hardly be stated, that *the success of any one council depends to a large degree on the competence of the executive director and his dedicated commitment to the organization and regionalism.*[41]

Similar to executive directors, most of the members of the professional staff of councils are planners, although a considerable number have academic backgrounds in public administration, civil engineering, economics, sociology, and law enforcement planning.[42] About twenty-five percent of staff time is spent on developing regional plans, with the balance of time allocated primarily to providing technical assistance to member governments, assisting local governments in preparing applications for federal grants, and providing other visible services to member governments.[43]

## Council Budgets
## and Fiscal Resources

When councils of governments first made their appearance in the fifties and early sixties their funding was of a minimal nature. The Supervisors' Inter-County Committee (SICC) had a total budget of $32,000 for the 1955 fiscal year.[44] The 1957 budget of the Puget Sound Governmental Conference (PSGC) was about $15,000.[45] The Metropolitan Washington Council of Governments (COG) reported spending about $9,400 in 1960.[46] In 1962, the average council budget was about $30,000, ranging from a low in total expenditures of about $14,000 to a high of approximately $67,000.[47] The limited financial resources of councils of governments during this period hindered their development and functional activity.

Councils currently enjoy considerably better funding than during the earlier period. For example, the 1974-75 fiscal budget of the Southern California Association of Governments (SCAG) was between $1,500,000 and $2,000,000;[48] during the same period the Metropolitan Washington Council of Governments (COG) had a budget of almost $5,000,000.[49] The Association of Bay Area Governments (ABAG) reported a budget of about $1,500,000[50] for the 1975 fiscal year. For the same year the

Puget Sound Governmental Conference (PSGC) spent about $1,590,000,[51] while the Southeast Michigan Council of Governments (SEMCOG) indicated expenditures of approximately $2,100,000.[52] A study compiled in 1970 found that the typical budget of regional councils ranged from $100,000 to $200,000.[53]

Councils of governments derive most of their funding from three basic sources: (1) federal grants, (2) general state support and grants, and (3) membership dues and contributions. In addition, some councils in the past have been the recipients of monies from private sources. The expansion of council budgets is primarily due to the increase of federal grants for various programmatic activities and general support for these bodies. About fifty to sixty percent of any one council's fiscal resources are derived from federal grants.[54] Federal programs that provide funding for regional councils include, but are not limited to: comprehensive planning assistance, (accounting for about forty-three percent of all federal funding for councils in the 1971 fiscal year[55]), water-sewer planning, highway planning, solid-waste disposal, economic development, comprehensive health planning, area pollution control, and water-quality management. Where applicable, approximately five to ten percent of each council's financial resources are derived from the state.[56] Fifteen states provide general financial support for councils; annual state allocations for each council typically vary from $3,000 to $50,000.[57] About twenty-six percent of all regional councils receive state financial assistance.[58] Given the present limited amount of state financial aid for councils, one can reasonably expect that financial support for these bodies from this level of government will increase in the future.

Membership dues and contributions, on the average, constitute about thirty to forty percent of the revenues of a regional council.[59] These funds are usually utilized to pay for general expenses and to provide matching funds for federal grants. Councils employ various formulas for determining council membership dues. A study conducted in 1967 found that councils assessed their members in the following diverse ways: (1) forty-five percent utilized a population (per capita) standard; (2) seven percent mandated a uniform membership fee for all members; (3) seven percent based their membership dues on assessed property valuation; (4) two percent utilized a formula based on a uniform fee plus population; (5) four percent assigned an arbitrary or negotiated amount; (6) twenty-one percent employed some combination of the above methods; and (7) fourteen percent utilized other approaches for determining the financial obligation of each member.[60] A study conducted in 1972 found that regional councils utilized the following methods for determining local membership fees: (1) three percent mandated a standard uniform fee; (2) three percent charged a standard fee for each *type* (i.e., municipality or county) of governmental jurisdiction; (3) fifty-eight percent employed a dues schedule based on population; (4) ten percent utilized some combination of the above methods; (5) thirteen percent employed a formula based on property valuation; and (6) the remainder utilized some other method for determining local membership fees.[61] Councils of governments, seeking to be somewhat less dependent on federal funding, are making concerted efforts to enlarge the amount of monies derived from their members.

## Summary and Conclusions

We can conclude this chapter by noting several general observations about the formation and characteristics of councils of governments. In general, council formation, usually enlisting the efforts of a small number of individuals, engenders little political conflict or controversy in the metropolis; this is partially due to the advisory and voluntary nature of councils. Councils have been relatively successful in attracting to their membership ranks most eligible governmental units. Further, only a limited number of members have terminated their council affiliation. In terms of organizational structure, practically all councils have a general assembly, in which each member has at *least* one representative, although the making of specific council policy is usually the responsibility of the executive board. An executive director, supported by appropriate staff, is retained to direct the day-to-day activities of the council; it seems clear that the success of any one council of governments is, to a substantial degree, dependent upon the competence and dedication of the executive director and staff.

# Notes

1. Information contained in this paragraph was drawn from sources cited in footnote b of Table 6.
2. Merged with the Capitol Region Planning Agency, 1974.
3. Interview with Dana Hansen, Manager for Regional Development, Greater Hartford Chamber of Commerce, August 8, 1967.
4. Interview with Walter Aston, Chairman, Capitol Region Council of Elected Officials, August 10, 1967.
5. For example, see William N. Cassella, Jr., "Town Meeting Held in Greater Hartford," *National Civic Review* 54 (January 1965): 591-593.
6. Royce Hanson, *Metropolitan Councils of Governments* (Washington, D.C.: Advisory Commission on Intergovernmental Relations, 1966), p. 6.
7. Interview with Robert Killian, Democratic Town Chairman, Hartford, June 27, 1967.
8. Jesse Unruh, speech, University of Connecticut, May 1, 1967. One should note that the author did not have a full discussion with Unruh concerning this matter.

9. Letter from Larry Pelughoeft, Assistant Director, Government Services, Puget Sound Governmental Conference, to the author, December 24, 1974.

10. Within a year of its formation twenty-nine of the eligible thirty-one localities were members of the Capitol Region Council of Elected Officials (CRCEO).

11. For a good discussion on the regional perspective, see Kent Mathewson, "A Regional Ethic," in *The Regionalist Papers,* ed. Kent Mathewson (Detroit: Metropolitan Fund, 1974), pp. 41-51.

12. Interview with Chester A. Kunz, Executive Director, Regional Conference of Elected Officials, June 6, 1967.

13. Interview with Mahlon P. Avery, First Selectman, Somers, Connecticut, July 21, 1966.

14. Interview with Donald Ilg, Town Manager, Windsor, Connecticut, August 23, 1966.

15. Interview with John Yeager, Republican party Town Chairman, Windsor, Connecticut, September 1, 1966.

16. William N. Cassella, Jr., "ABAG Suggested as Area Planning Agency," *National Civic Review* 51 (November 1962): 573.

17. Institute for Local Self Government, *ABAG Appraised: A Quinquennial Review of Voluntary Regional Cooperative Action Through the Association of Bay Area Governments* (Berkeley, Calif.: The Institute, 1965), p. 39.

18. Association of Bay Area Governments, *ABAG* (Berkeley, Calif: The Association, 1974), p. 1.

19. Letter from Barton R. Meays, Deputy Executive Director, Southern California Association of Governments, to the author, November 7, 1974.

20. Telephone conversation with James Thomas, information service officer, Southeast Michigan Council of Governments, July 24, 1975.

21. Advisory Commission on Intergovernmental Relations, *Regional Decision Making: New Strategies for Substate Districts* (Washington, D.C.: The Commission, 1973), p. 265. One should note that the average figures presented relate to *regional councils in general*, not specifically to councils of governments in particular.

22. Ibid., p. 87.

23. Ibid.

24. Ibid., p. 88. See also Stephen L. Garmen, "COGs '72: A Central City View: Coordination Instead of Competition," *Nation's Cities* 10 (November 1972): 30-32.
25. Ibid., p. 82.
26. Charles W. Harris, *Regional COG's and the Central City* (Detroit: Metropolitan Fund, Inc., 1970), p. 6.
27. Ibid.
28. Advisory Commission on Intergovernmental Relations, *Regional Decision Making,* p. 82.
29. Information relating to the organizational structure of SCAG was derived from Southern California Association of Governments, *Annual Report '73* (Los Angeles: The Association, 1973).
30. Joseph F. Zimmerman, "Metropolitan Ecumenism: The Road to the Promised Land?" *Journal of Urban Law* 44 (Spring 1967): 447.
31. Interview with Glenn E. Bennett, Secretary, Metropolitan Atlanta Council of Local Governments, June 13, 1967.
32. Advisory Commission on Intergovernmental Relations, *Regional Decision Making,* p. 94.
33. Metropolitan Washington Council of Governments, *Goals, Objectives, and Work Program for Greater Washington: An Overall Program Design for the Metropolitan Washington Council of Governments, 1974-1976* (Washington, D.C.: The Council, 1974), p. 75.
34. Meays to the author, November 7, 1974.
35. Association of Bay Area Governments, *ABAG,* p. 1.
36. Pelughoeft to author, December 24, 1974.
37. Laurie S. Frankel and Walter A. Scheiber, "Characteristics and Administrative Relationships of Regional Council Directors," *Urban Data Service, International City Management Association* 5 (October 1973): 4.
38. Ibid., pp. 1-2.
39. Advisory Commission on Intergovernmental Relations, *Regional Decision Making,* p. 95.
40. Frankel and Scheiber, "Characteristics and Administrative Relationships," p. 5.
41. Interview with Walter A. Scheiber, Executive Director, Metropolitan Washington Council of Governments (COG), November 27, 1974.

42. Advisory Commission on Intergovernmental Relations, *Regional Decision Making,* p. 95.
43. Frankel and Scheiber, "Characteristics and Administrative Relationships," p. 5.
44. Interview with Gerard H. Coleman, Executive Director, Supervisors' Inter-County Committee, June 16, 1967.
45. Puget Sound Governmental Conference, *Puget Sound Governmental Conference: A Synopsis* (Seattle: The Conference, 1966), p. 1.
46. Royce Hanson, *The Politics of Metropolitan Cooperation: Metropolitan Washington Council of Governments* (Washington, D.C.: Washington Center for Metropolitan Studies, 1964), p. 11.
47. Advisory Commission on Intergovernmental Relations, *Regional Decision Making,* p. 60.
48. Meays to author, November 7, 1974.
49. Metropolitan Washington Council of Governments, *Goals, Objectives, and Work Program,* p. 21.
50. Association of Bay Area Governments, *ABAG,* p. 1.
51. Pelughoeft to author, December 24, 1974.
52. Thomas conversation, July 24, 1975.
53. National Association of Regional Councils, *Action Through Intergovernmental Cooperation* (Washington, D.C.: The Association, 1972), p. 5.
54. Ibid.
55. Advisory Commission on Intergovernmental Relations, *Regional Decision Making,* p. 90.
56. National Association of Regional Councils, *Action Through Intergovernmental Cooperation,* p. 5.
57. National Service to Regional Councils, *Regionalism: A New Dimension in Local Government and Intergovernmental Relations* (Washington, D.C.: The Service, 1971), p. 12.
58. Ibid.
59. National Association of Regional Councils, *Action Through Intergovernmental Cooperation,* p. 5.
60. National Service to Regional Councils, *Regionalism,* p. 13.
61. Advisory Commission on Intergovernmental Relations, *Regional Decision Making,* p. 90.

# The Activities and
# Functional Concerns
# of Councils
# of Governments

**4**

Councils of governments engage in a number of diverse activities and functions. These activities may be grouped into four broad categories: (1) serving as a forum for the discussion of common and regional problems and approaches to be adopted for alleviating these problems; (2) physical and social regional planning and, through planning, facilitating joint cooperation between localities; (3) representing their members before appropriate state administrative and legislative bodies, and providing them with assorted technical services; and (4) serving as a regional review agency for the federal government to assess whether local projects submitted for federal funding are consistent and compatible with regional needs.

## Forum of Discussion

The initial and most salient function of a council of governments is that of serving as a forum of discussion where like chief elected officials, i.e., mayors, can periodically come together to discuss common and regional problems. As long ago as 1963, William Cassella, Jr., wrote in the *National Civic Review:*

> They [councils] seek a better understanding among the governments and officials in the area, to develop a consensus regarding metropolitan needs and to promote coordinated action in solving their problems. . . . They are a means by which strong units of local government may work together cooperatively to determine region-wide comprehensive policies and to accomplish the programs implementing these policies.[1]

Council meetings perform the very important function of acquainting and familiarizing elected public officials with their counterparts throughout the region. Rather than beginning meetings of councils being a gathering of friends, they are in reality composed of relative strangers. Allen Long notes of the initial meeting of the Metropolitan Washington Council of Governments (COG), "The first meeting attracted 40 persons. It began with each person introducing himself, for mostly those people were mutual strangers."[2] The late Gerard Coleman, former executive director of the Supervisors' Inter-County Committee (SICC), noted:

> When the members of SICC first came together the people of Wayne [County] sat at one table, the people of Macomb [County] sat at another table, and those from Oakland [County] sat at still another [table]. This was understandable for the people of the different counties did not know each other. . . . It was only after a period of time that they began to mix with each other.[3]

Similarly, Walter Aston, the first Chairman of the Capitol Region Council of Election Officials (CRCEO), of the Hartford, Connecticut area, commenting upon the introductory meetings of that council of governments asserted:

> Oh, at the first few meetings of the Council we didn't do much more than have the members get to know each other. You see, when the members first got together, they were practically total strangers. They had never seen each other before.

Aston went on to state:

> It was only after the members had gotten to know each other that they began to realize that most of the localities were beset by many of the same problems. . . . And the small-towns' delegates began to lose some of their fear of the central city. You know, after the small-town delegates met Corrigan [the representative of Hartford to the Council], they realized he was no monster.[4]

Especially during the nascent period of council development, it is important that no one locality dominates or is perceived by the other members as dominating the discussion sessions and other activities of the organization. Regarding this point, Royce Hanson has written:

> One element does seem important during the formative stages of the organization. That element is confidence by the member governments that no one locality or group of units is using the organization to further its own special interests at the expense of the rest of the area.[5]

Mindful of the above, councils of governments have usually taken particular efforts to ensure that the core city of the region does not dominate council agenda; indeed, one might well argue that councils, on occasions, have adopted special measures designed to placate the fears of suburbanites. Illustrative of this, Kent Mathewson, a former representative of Salem, Oregon, to the Mid-Willamette Valley Council of Governments (M-WVCOG) stated:

> When we had our meetings it was always I who went to their courthouses and other places [seats of governments], they [suburbanites] never usually came to Salem. . . . I doubt

that we ever had more than a couple of meetings in Salem. . . . I had to be careful. . . . I could not give them grounds to think that Salem intended to dominate the council.[6]

Philadelphia was a founding member of the ill-fated Regional Council of Elected Officials (RCEO); several of the mayors of that community played strong roles in that organization. Nevertheless, to assure the other members of RCEO that the agenda of the organization was not unduly shaped by the consideration of core-city interests, the leadership roles of the mayors of Philadelphia had to be portrayed as somewhat less visible:

Oh, yes, the mayors of Philadelphia have been very active members of the Council [RCEO]. But we have had to sort of play that down. The suburbanites would get suspicious. Dilworth [mayor of Philadelphia when RCEO was first organized] understood that very well. But when Tate [the succeeding Mayor] first came in, I [executive director] had a little trouble. All of a sudden there were a lot of statements coming out of Tate's office regarding the council. I got in contact with Tate and discussed the matter . . . told him how the suburbanites would react. He agreed [for the good of the organization] to cut down on the number of press releases regarding the Council. . . . Everything has been all right since.[7]

Councils of governments have functioned rather successfully as forums for the discussion of common and regional problems. This is particularly true of councils that are composed of a limited membership where the representatives of all the governmental units come together on a fairly regular basis. A study conducted jointly by the Advisory Commission on Intergovernmental Relations (ACIR) and the International City Management Association (ICMA) found that local officials generally agreed that through council deliberations and other ways these organizations had enhanced communication among local officials, improved general local-government coordination, and generated new ideas about local problems.[8] Specifically, council forum sessions have served to mitigate core-city and suburban political conflict and distrust. Finally, council discourse has given additional credence and legitimacy to the concept of regionalism; reflective of this Walter Scheiber, executive director of the Metropolitan Washington Council of Governments, noted, "I remember when a politician supported COG at his or her political peril. It was felt to be antilocal. There has been a change in the tide. Now people run as affirmed proponents of regionalism."[9]

## Regional Physical and
## Social Planning Activities

Councils of governments are involved in various general and specific regional planning endeavors. At minimum, all councils are involved in general comprehensive planning with an increasing emphasis in these plans devoted to social needs and human concerns, rather than simply physical considerations. In addition, councils, largely through federal stimulus, have become involved in a myriad array of specific functional planning activities. The Housing and Development Act of 1968 mandated that all councils that receive "701" comprehensive planning assistance—practically all councils do—are required to prepare so-called "initial housing elements." These working papers are to document the supply and demand for housing throughout the region, the obstacles or barriers to new housing construction, and policies to be employed to meet regional housing needs. A study conducted by the National Association of Regional Councils (NARC) in 1972 found that about three-quarters of all regional councils were involved in housing planning.[10]

Several council regional planning efforts in the area of housing are particularly noteworthy. The Centre Regional

Council of Governments of the State College, Pennsylvania area, developed the first regional comprehensive code-enforcement program in the country. This program includes five areas of code enforcement: building, plumbing, housing, electrical, and fire prevention.[11] The Metropolitan Washington Council of Governments (COG) has adopted a "fair-share" housing plan, similar to the Dayton plan,[12] for the distribution of low-income public housing throughout the greater Washington area.[13]

As a result of the passage of the Federal Aid Highway Act of 1962, which stipulated that highway projects would not generate federal funding unless they were the product of a continuing comprehensive regional process, many councils have become involved in highway, as well as mass transportation planning. In 1972, it was found that approximately sixty-six percent of all regional councils had officially adopted a transportation plan or policy.[14] The East-West Coordinating Council of the St. Louis metropolitan area, the Regional Council of Elected Officials of South Central Connecticut, and the Southern California Association of Governments, to cite several examples, have been selected by the Department of Transportation to receive funding for transportation project planning designed to alleviate urban traffic congestion.[15] The Metropolitan Washington Council of Governments (COG) has been especially active in regional transportation planning. In the recent past, it has been involved in planning and implementing various transportation projects, including express lanes on highways for early morning and evening vehicle commuter traffic, and express and dial-a-ride bus programs for the Washington region.[16]

Some councils of governments have moved into the area of regional law-enforcement planning; in 1972 it was found that forty-four percent of the regional councils had adopted a law-enforcement plan or policy.[17] COG law-

enforcement planning has to a major extent been supported by funds made available by the Omnibus Crime
Control and Safe Streets Act passed by Congress in 1968,
and routed through the states. Further, the former Metropolitan Atlanta Council of Local Governments (MAC-
LOG) and the Metropolitan Washington Council of
Governments (COG) have each developed mutual-aid
police agreements; further, one might note that the Concho
Valley Council of Governments, of the San Angelo, Texas,
area has successfully planned and developed a system of
mutual-aid fire-fighting arrangements.[18]

Council planning efforts in other areas have served to
stimulate greater horizontal intergovernmental cooperation. A number of councils have designed joint purchasing
programs; one of the first councils that did so was the Mid-
Willamette Valley Council of Governments (M-WVCOG),
developing a program of this nature in the late fifties.[19] The
Southeast Michigan Council of Governments (SEMCOG)
estimates that its members save a total of more than
$50,000 each year through the cooperative purchasing plan
it designed and implemented.[20] M-WVCOG has promoted
greater regional cooperation among the libraries of the
area.[21] The Pikes Peak Area Council of Governments, of
the Colorado Springs region, has planned a cooperative
computer program for the benefit of its members.[22]

Over the years, councils of governments have engaged
in a wide-ranging array of environmental planning activities. In the early sixties, the Supervisors' Inter-County
Committee (SICC) conducted several studies relating to
water and sewer facilities; currently more than eighty
percent of the councils have approved a regional water-
sewer plan.[23] The Metropolitan Washington Council of
Governments (COG) planned and facilitated the implementation of the first regional landfill operation.[24] The
former Regional Council of Elected Officials (RCEO) of the

Philadelphia region, the North Central Texas Council of Governments, the Metropolitan Washington Council of Governments (COG), and the Denver Regional Council of Governments were among the first councils to engage in quality-air planning.[25] In 1966, COG developed a model air-pollution ordinance that was adopted and implemented by eleven cities and six counties in the area by 1970; as an outgrowth of this planning activity COG provides an air polution advisory service for the citizenry of the region.[26] The Denver Regional Council of Governments drafted model air-pollution regulations in 1965; these regulations were adopted by twenty-one of the thirty-eight governmental jurisdictions in the region by 1968.[27] In addition, it should be noted that by 1972 three-quarters of all regional councils had adopted a regional open-space/recreation plan;[28] the large number of councils that have a plan of this nature is partially accounted for by the requirement that all councils that receive "701" funds are directed to formulate open-space plans.

More recently, some councils of governments have moved into other diverse areas of regional human and social planning. These areas most prominently include health, manpower, and economic development. Council planning in these areas has been encouraged by federal support and funding assistance.

A number of observations may be advanced concerning the regional planning endeavors of councils of governments. First, the planning agenda of councils has been shaped to a marked degree by the availability of federal funding; many councils have done a minimum of planning in those areas where federal requirements or funding are absent. This raises the real possibility that perhaps council planning efforts are unduly structured by the availability of federal funding, as opposed to what might be the real needs and problems of the region.

Second, in contrast to the early years of council development, these organizations are becoming decidedly more involved in social, as opposed to physical, planning efforts. Nevertheless, councils, reflective of their often consensual orientation, are perceived by local officials as being more successful in carrying out their physical, as opposed to social, planning endeavors.[29] And finally, councils of governments have enjoyed only limited success in implementing, in a programmatic fashion, their planning efforts, a problem, of course, not unique to these organizations.

## Other Functional Activities

In addition to carrying on various planning activities, councils of governments have conducted assorted functional activities of benefit to their members. This summation of the various functional activities of councils is not designed to be exhaustive or all-inclusive, but rather representative and to simply illustrate the wide range and diversity of council activities.

For some years, councils have presented the views of their members on •various concerns and issues before appropriate state legislative and executive officials. As long ago as 1964, William Cassella, Jr., wrote regarding the interaction of the Association of Bay Area Governments (ABAG) with higher levels of government:

> ABAG is . . . dealing itself in on federal-state negotiations and enabling local governments in the Bay area as a unit to play a new and important role in intergovernmental relations. Initially aiding joint action among local governments, ABAG is now extending its scope to include negotiations with higher levels.[30]

Similarly, the first executive director of the former Supervisors' Inter-County Committee (SICC) noted:

> Oh yes, I go to Lansing [to the state legislature] and appear before many legislative bodies on behalf of SICC. It is an

important responsibility of mine. You know, when I go there they are aware that I represent all of the six counties in the Detroit area. You see, the council does not take a stand on any issue without the consent of all its members. . . . Hence, I can speak for the entire Detroit region . . . and they listen.[31]

Through this representational activity, councils have served to further build channels of articulation and communication between their members and state officials.

Councils of governments have long been involved in providing their members with technical and training assistance. This might well be labeled as the "service" activity of councils. The Concho Valley COG, in the San Angelo, Texas, region has provided localities with assistance and guidance in upgrading firefighting procedures and practices, in addition to furnishing advice regarding equipment-improvement needs.[32] The Association of Central Oklahoma Governments (Oklahoma City), the North Central Texas Council of Governments, and the former Metropolitan Atlanta Council of Local Governments have operated regional training programs for criminal justice and law enforcement personnel.[33] The Heart of Texas Council of Governments (Waco, Texas) developed a laboratory on crime prevention that provides training to the appropriate officials of the more than sixty school districts of the area.[34] The North Central Texas Council of Governments has implemented an on-the-job training program for waste-water treatment-plant operators.[35] The Metropolitan Washington Council of Governments (COG) currently operates a training program for housing-authority staffs and housing inspectors in the region.[36]

Councils of governments perform an important role in providing internship experience for members of minority groups contemplating a career in the public sector. The Metropolitan Washington Council of Governments (COG), the East-West Coordinating Council, the Southeast Michigan Council of Governments (SEMCOG), and the Southern California Association of Governments (SCAG) have each received funding from the Department of Housing and Urban Development to provide work-study projects for members of minority groups designed to supplement their academic training in planning and related areas.[37]

## Regional Review Agency

One of the more salient activities of councils of governments is that of serving as a regional review agency for the federal government. Section 204 of the Demonstration Cities and Metropolitan Development Act of 1966 gave official sanction to the policy that at least some local projects to be financed partially by federal funding should be reviewed by an area-wide agency to ascertain if the proposed project was compatible with the regional needs and plan of the area. Section 204 provided that after June 30, 1967, all applications for over thirty federal grant or loan programs to assist certain types of public works planning and construction activities, and for open-space acquisition, "shall be submitted for review to any area-wide agency which is designated to perform metropolitan or regional planning for the area within which the assistance is to be employed. . . ."[38] Such applications for Federal assistance were to be accompanied by: (1) the comments and recommendations of the area-wide agency regarding the proposed project and (2) a statement by the applicant acknowledging that such comments and recommendations had been considered prior to the formal submission of the application. Although general administrative oversight for "204" review was initially lodged with the Department of Housing and Urban Development, this responsibility was transferred to the then Bureau of the Budget in December, 1967, now the Office of Management and Budget (OMB).

The "204" review requirement was obliquely responsible for the proliferation of councils of governments during the late sixties.

A total of 3060 "204" project reviews for federal agencies were conducted by councils of governments and other, primarily regional planning commissions, area-wide bodies in 1968; in 1969 this number was 3134. In both years the largest number of reviews (1453 in 1968; 1114 in 1969) were forwarded to the Department of Housing and Urban Development. The Department of Transportation was the recipient of the second largest number of reviews, totaling 856 in 1968 and 912 in 1969. Hence, more than half of the total "204" reviews in each calendar year were received by the two aforementioned agencies. Reviews were also conducted for the Departments of Interior, Agriculture, Commerce, and Health, Education, and Welfare, along with the Army Corps of Engineers.[39]

These "204" reviews concerned various functional areas. In both 1968 and 1969, approximately one-third of all reviews involved water, sewer, and waste-treatment projects; the second largest number of reviews involved highway projects. Other reviewed projects involved open space, urban planning, public-works planning, airports, hospitals and health, and additional assorted functional areas. The overwhelming majority of "204" reviews conducted by councils and other area-wide agencies were favorable; only five percent of the reviews in 1968 and eighteen percent completed in 1969 recommended project changes.[40] Nevertheless, the "204" requirement established the precedent and developed a rudimentary structure for area-wide review. According to a study issued by the former Bureau of the Budget, the most significant contribution made by the "204" review requirement ". . . was an increased level of interlocal communication and cooperation in metropolitan areas."[41]

The regional review function and responsibility of

councils of governments were significantly enhanced by the passage of the Intergovernmental Cooperation Act of 1968. Title IV of this legislation states:

> The President shall . . . establish rules and regulations governing the formulation, evaluation, and review of federal programs and projects having a significant impact on area and community development. . . . All viewpoints—nation, regional, state, and local—shall, to the extent possible, be fully considered and taken into account in planning federal or federally assisted development programs and projects. . . . To the maximum extent possible, consistent with national objectives, all federal aid for development purposes shall be consistent with and further the objectives of state, regional, and local comprehensive planning.[42]

Circular A-95 issued by the Office of Management and Budget on July 24, 1969, implemented the above legislation. As one scholar has noted regarding this document:

> This circular sought to stimulate a network of state, regional, and metropolitan planning and development clearinghouses to receive and disseminate information about proposed projects; to coordinate between applicants for federal assistance; to act as a liaison between federal agencies contemplating federal development projects, and to conduct an evaluation of the state, regional, or metropolitan significance of federal or federally assisted projects.[43]

The original A-95 circular expanded to about fifty the number of federally aided projects required to be submitted for review to an area-wide agency. In addition to the "brick and mortar" projects previously designated for review under Section 204, the above document added planning assistance programs for health care, law enforcement and juvenile delinquency control, community action, and economic development.

In several subsequent revisions of A-95, the Office of Management and Budget (OMB) has broadened the review process to include additional federal programs. For instance, on February 9, 1971, OMB mandated that housing and urban renewal, model cities, educational facilities, mental-health facilities, and law-enforcement action grants were subject to area-wide review. In the same revised circular, councils of governments and other review agencies were assigned the responsibility of determining the environmental impact of a variety of local projects. This additional responsibility flowed from the implementation of Section 102 (2)(c) of the National Environmental Policy Act of 1969 that requires Federal agencies to submit to the Council of Environmental Quality information on projects affecting the environment. In addition, the 1971 revision of A-95 mandated that for certain HUD housing assistance and mortgage insurance programs developers are to submit directly to HUD a preliminary application containing a brief description of the project. A copy of the "feasibility analysis" part of the application is then sent to the review agency, which has fifteen days to make comments concerning the project to HUD.[44]

Several revisions were made of the A-95 Circular in 1972 and 1973. On March 8, 1972, the document was amended to mandate that review agencies are to provide agencies responsible for enforcing civil-rights laws the opportunity to ". . . review the civil rights aspects of the proposed project and make comments and recommendations on the extent to which it contributed to balanced settlement patterns and service delivery systems affecting minority groups and to housing opportunities for all segments of the community."[45] Toward the end of 1973, the Office of Management and Budget (OMB) expanded the A-95 review to include many social programs of the Departments of Labor and Health, Education, and Welfare. Hence, approximately 150 federally aided programs are presently subject to "clearinghouse" review.[46]

Part 1 of Circular A-95 establishes a Project Notification and Review System (PNRS), which is built upon the previous "204" review process. The operation of this "early-warning system" is presented in diagram form in Chart 3. Under this system all state and local agencies that have opted to apply for a federally assisted development project covered by the circular are required to inform the appropriate council of governments—about 390 councils have been designated as A-95 "clearinghouses"—or other review body of their intention. Further, the applicant is required to provide the reviewing agency with a brief description of the project and the date that the application will be submitted to the appropriate federal agency for possible funding. At this point, the "clearinghouse" has thirty days to indicate its own or other state or local interest in the proposed project and to arrange a conference with the applicant and concerned parties to discuss issues and resolve any possible conflicts. If the project raises no issues or if the problems are resolved in conference the clearinghouse "signs off," i.e., forwards the application to the appropriate federal agency. If the issues or conflicts are not resolved, the clearinghouse forwards its comments along with those registered by any other state or local agencies to the applicant who in turn submits the application along with the comments to the federal funding agency. What should be stressed is that the area-wide review process is only of an *advisory* nature; federal agencies are not bound by the recommendations of the area-wide review body. However, it appears clear that if a council of governments writes a "negative" review of a project the prospect of federal funding for the same is considerably diminished.[47]

In reviewing a project application, the council may make comments in nine areas regarding the consistency of the proposed project with state, regional, and local comprehensive plans and federal laws:

(1) appropriate land uses, (2) wise development and conservation of natural resources, (3) balanced transportation systems, (4) adequate outdoor recreation and open

## CHART 3
### REGIONAL PROJECT NOTIFICATION AND REVIEW SYSTEM[a]

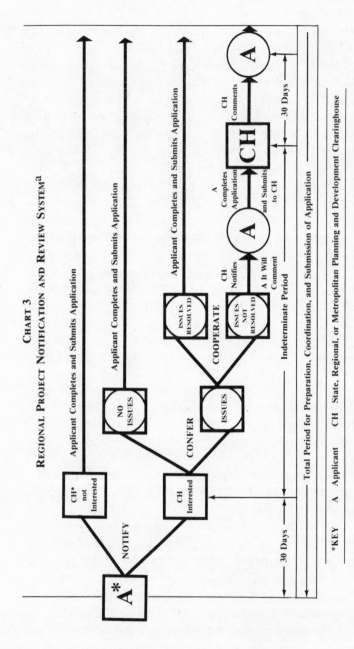

a *Source:* Advisory Commission on Intergovernmental Relations, *Regional Decision Making: New Strategies for Substate Districts* (Washington, D.C.: The Commission, 1973), 146.

*KEY    A   Applicant      CH   State, Regional, or Metropolitan Planning and Development Clearinghouse spaces, (5) protection of areas of unique natural beauty and historical and scientific interest, (6) properly planned community facilities, (7) high design standards, (8) environmental impact, and (9) balanced settlement patterns and delivery services to all sectors of the population, including minority groups.[48]

Pursuant to the requirements of A-95, councils of governments and other designated area-wide agencies have reviewed a considerable number of local projects submitted for possible federal funding. In 1973, the Association of Bay Area Governments (ABAG) considered 426 project applications amounting to nearly $302 million in project costs; from January to June of 1974, the same council reviewed project applications involving an aggregate cost of nearly $323 million.[49] In 1973, the Metropolitan Washington Council of Governments (COG) reviewed local projects that involved about $8.6 billion in federal funds.[50] In 1970, the National Association of Regional Councils (NARC) asserted that regional councils serving as "clearinghouses" reviewed more than $15.5 billion dollars of project applications and saved the taxpayers an estimated 300 million dollars.[51] NARC notes that in 1971 review agencies reviewed local projects valued at approximately 25 billion dollars and saved $483 million in public funds.[52] Whether these savings are real savings or only "paper" savings is a matter of conjecture since one federal official has noted:

*From the Federal standpoint, it is doubtful if any actual savings have been achieved from the operation of clearinghouses. Certainly, the weeding out of bad projects results in the avoidance of waste and the reviews of the clearinghouses help to establish priorities. However, for most Federal grant programs, more applications are received than there are funds available in any given year. Thus the effect of clearinghouse actions does not directly reduce even the aggravation cost of operating the program.[53]

Further, on the average, only in the instance of about one out of every ten applications do councils write a critical or negative review to accompany the local application being submitted to a federal agency.[54] This is partially due, on the one hand, to the general high quality of project applications and sometimes, on the other, to the absence of area-wide plans or other criteria for evaluating proposals. Further, the low rate of critical reviews is due to the limited staff, funds, and time that many councils can afford to devote to this function. Despite the importance of the A-95 review function, one study found that about seventy-five percent of the councils expended only about ten percent of their staff time to A-95 review, and eighty-five percent of the councils allocated ten percent or less of their total budget for this activity.[55]

The rather low percentage of instances in which councils opt to write a critical or negative review of a local project is not necessarily a good indicator or measure of the effectiveness and utility of the A-95 review process. As one study asserts:

> Another important factor (accounting for the low percentage of negative reviews) is the informal considera-tion and modification of projects before they enter the formal review process. It has been argued that after the major tradeoffs and compromises are made at this stage, and that in the absence of the A-95 requirement these adjustments probably would not take place. This contention is supported by the questionnaire replies: As a result of informal A-95 staff activities, 58 percent of 22 clearing-houses indicated that substantial changes had been made in project applications, and 40 percent of 202 agencies stated that applications had been withdrawn.[56]

A number of studies have been made regarding the merits and effectiveness of the A-95 review process. A study carried out by the International City Management Association (ICMA) in 1971 found that municipal and county officials believe the primary accomplishments of the A-95 review process include: (1) increased intergovernmental coordination, (2) the provision of useful information, (3) the promotion of orderly development, (4) feedback to federal agencies, and (5) the identification of possible project conflicts.[57] In the same year, a report issued by the Council of State Governments asserted of the A-95 review process:

> In general, the PNRS and clearinghouses have been well-received and are operating effectively in providing project-by-project planning and coordination. At both State and area-wide levels, clearinghouses are identifying potential conflicts, duplication and ineffectiveness in proposed expenditures of Federal grant-in-aid funds. In some cases, clearinghouses have become actively involved in the specifics of project planning; lending staff expertise toward better grant application and project operation.[58]

Melvin B. Mogulof, formerly of the Urban Institute, conducted a comparative on-the-site evaluation of the A-95 review process and reported his findings in *Governing Metropolitan Areas: A Critical Review of Council of Governments and the Federal Role.*[59] According to Mogulof, the achievements of the A-95 review process include: (1) alerting the council to proposed local actions seeking federal funds and initiating a sophisticated clearance system, (2) informing local officials about the availability of federal funds, (3) providing council technical assistance to members, and (4) making local general purpose government into a larger local clearinghouse for federal activity in its area.[60]

The main shortcoming of the A-95 review process, concluded Mogulof, is the often inability of councils to distinguish "between good and bad applications from a regional point of view."[61] He notes that: "In the clearinghouses we observed we know of no action taken under the A-95 review process which could be construed as harmful to a local government on an important issue."[62] Other failures include: (1) the failure of some federal agencies to demonstrate any interest in the process or take into consideration the issues that some councils advance about an application, (2) the failure by some federal agencies to inform the council about whether a grant has been made, (3) the inability of some councils to insist on review prerogratives when a major governmental member wants to rush an application through, (4) the tendency of some councils to review an application because of its potential effectiveness rather than for its implications for regional coordination and the realization of regional goals, (5) a tendency for reviews to be idiosyncratic, rather than based upon established policy, and (6) an often lack of site visiting by council staff to applicant communities.[63]

Mogulof concluded his evaluation of the A-95 review process by stating:

> In sum, the achievements of the A-95 process are real and important. They would appear to offer ready validation for the survival and growth of the clearinghouse concept. But the failures of the A-95 process are equally real and important.[64]

To be sure, the A-95 review process has not worked perfectly; given the often consensual nature of council bodies and their dependence on their member units we can hardly expect that this process will be carried out significantly better in the future. Nevertheless, the A-95 process has engendered greater regional coordination and made local governments more conscious of regional considerations and needs. Through the former "204" and A-95 process the federal government has begun the task of building, although rudimentary, some measure of regional structure into the planning process.

## Summary and Conclusions

We can conclude this chapter by asserting that councils of governments are performing a variety of useful functions in the metropolis. By serving as forums of discussion, councils have been able to identify common and regional problems, and at least, in some instances, to persuade local governments to adopt unified policies to deal with these problems. Councils, then, have been somewhat successful in promoting a regional, as opposed to a local, point of view. Further, these bodies have provided varied general and technical assistance to their members and engendered greater horizontal as well as vertical governmental cooperation. Through their regional planning efforts and by serving as A-95 review agencies, councils are ensuring a more orderly and rational development of our regional areas.

# Notes

1. William Cassella, Jr., "Local Governments Cooperate on Problems," *National Civic Review* 52 (April 1963): 214.
2. Allen Long, "Creative Self-Help Marks the D.C. Area's Councils of Governments," *Commonwealth* 37 (July 1970): 37.
3. Interview with Gerard H. Coleman, Executive Director, Supervisors' Inter-County Committee, June 16, 1967.
4. Interview with Walter Aston, Chairman, Capitol Region Council of Elected Officials, August 10, 1967.
5. Royce Hanson, *Metropolitan Councils of Governments* (Washington, D.C.: Advisory Commission on Intergovernmental Relations, 1966), p. 5.
6. Interview with Kent Mathewson, President, Metropolitan Fund, Detroit (formerly City Administrator of Salem, Oregon), June 15, 1967.
7. Interview with Chester A. Kunz, Executive Director, Regional Conference of Elected Officials, June 6, 1967.
8. Advisory Commission on Intergovernmental Relations, *Regional Decision Making: New Strategies for Substate Districts* (Washington, D.C.: The Commission, 1973), p. 121.
9. *The Washington Post,* 19 April 1973, p. G-1.
10. National Association of Regional Councils, "Regional

Councils: Action Through Intergovernmental Cooperation," in *Special Report* (Washington, D.C.: The Association, 1972), p. 2.

11. National Service to Regional Councils, *Regionalism: A New Dimension in Local Government and Intergovernmental Relations* (Washington, D.C.: The Service, 1971), p. 18.

12. *New York Times,* 17 November 1974, p. 67.

13. National Association of Regional Councils, "Wanted: A Decent Home in a Suitable Environment," in *Special Report* (Washington, D.C.: The Association, 1972), p. 9.

14. Advisory Commission on Intergovernmental Relations, *Regional Decision Making,* p. 96.

15. National Service to Regional Councils, "Wanted: Better Transportation Facilities," *Regional Review Quarterly* 4 (January 1971): 13.

16. National Service to Regional Councils, *Regionalism,* p. 18. 21, and *The Washington Post,* 22 October 1974, p. B-8.

17. Advisory Commission on Intergovernmental Relations, *Regional Decision Making,* p. 96.

18. National Service to Regional Councils, *Regionalism,* p. 19.

19. Roscoe Martin, "The Conference Approach: The Mid-Willamette Valley Council of Governments," in *Metropolis in Transition* (Washington, D.C.: U.S. Government Printing Office, 1963), p. 43.

20. National Service to Regional Councils, *Regionalism,* p. 18.

21. Martin, "The Conference Approach," p. 43.

22. National Association of Regional Councils, "Joint Services— Economy and Efficiency for Local Government," in *Special Report* (Washington, D.C.: The Association, 1972), p. 4.

23. Advisory Commission on Intergovernmental Relations, *Regional Decision Making,* p. 96.

24. National Association of Regional Councils, "Cleaning Up the Environment," in *Special Report* (Washington, D.C.: The Association, 1972), p. 8.

25. With reference to the Regional Council of Elected Officials, see William N. Cassella, Jr., "Air Pollution Control Stressed by RCEO," *National Civic Review* 51 (May 1962): 275-279.

26. National Service to Regional Councils, "Working for Clean Air and a Quality Environment," *Regional Review Quarterly* 4 (January 1971): 4.

27. Ibid.

28. Advisory Commission on Intergovernmental Relations, *Regional Decision Making*, p. 96.
29. Ibid., p. 121.
30. William N. Cassella, Jr., "ABAG to Develop Regional Solutions," *National Civic Review* 53 (December 1964): 607.
31. Coleman interview, June 16, 1967.
32. National Service to Regional Councils, "Faster Emergency Assistance Through Flexible Regional Councils," *Regional Review Quarterly* 4 (January 1971): 8.
33. National Service to Regional Councils, *Regionalism*, p. 19 and National Association of Regional Councils, "Relating Jobs to the Regional Market," in *Special Report* (Washington, D.C.: The Association, 1972), p. 17.
34. National Service to Regional Councils, "Crime and Juvenile Delinquency: A Regional Problem," *Regional Review Quarterly* 4 (January 1971): 8.
35. National Service to Regional Councils, *Regionalism*, p. 19.
36. National Service to Regional Councils, "Training Public Officials On a Regional Basis," *Regional Review Quarterly* 4 (January 1971): 17.
37. Ibid.
38. Melvin B. Mogulof, *Governing Metropolitan Areas: A Critical Review of Councils of Governments and the Federal Role* (Washington, D.C.: The Urban Institute, 1971), p. 5.
39. U.S. Executive Office of the President, Bureau of the Budget, "Section 204 of the Demonstration Cities and Metropolitan Development Act of 1966: Two Years' Experience," mimeographed (Washington, D.C.: The Bureau, April 10, 1970), p. 5.
40. Ibid., p. 9.
41. Ibid., p. 12.
42. Mogulof, *Governing Metropolitan Areas*, p. 5.
43. Ibid., p. 6.
44. Advisory Commission on Intergovernmental Relations, *Regional Decision Making*, pp. 145, 147.
45. Ibid., p. 147.
46. Norman Beckman, "Federal Policy for Metropolitan Governance," *National Civic Review* 63 (March 1974): 131.
47. Interview with Walter Scheiber, Executive Director of the Metropolitan Washington Council of Governments (COG), November 27, 1974.

48. Advisory Commission on Intergovernmental Relations, *Regional Decision Making*, p. 145.

49. Association of Bay Area Governments, *Program Capsule: A-95 Review Function Promotes Cooperation among Governments* (Berkeley, California: The Association, 1974), p. 3.

50. Metropolitan Washington Council of Governments, *Beyond the Handshake . . .* (Washington, D.C.: The Council, 1974).

51. National Service to Regional Councils, "Coordination Eliminates Conflicting Efforts," *Regional Review Quarterly* 4 (January 1971): 9.

52. National Association of Regional Councils, "What Regional Councils Are Doing, II," in *Special Report* (Washington, D.C.: The Association, 1972), p. 1.

53. Advisory Commission on Intergovernmental Relations, *Regional Decision Making*, p. 151.

54. Ibid., p. 148.

55. Ibid., p. 150.

56. Ibid., p. 149.

57. B. Douglas Harman, "Area-wide Review of Federal Grant Applications: Implications for Urban Management," *Urban Data Service* (Washington, D.C.: International City Management Association, 1972), pp. 12-13.

58. Council of State Governments, *Coming Together: The Intergovernmental Cooperation Act of 1968—Survey of Federal and State Implementation* (Washington, D.C.: The Council, 1971), p. 19.

59. Mogulof, *Governing Metropolitan Areas*, p. 6.

60. Ibid., pp. 49-50.

61. Ibid., p. 53.

62. Ibid., pp. 38-39.

63. Ibid., p. 54.

64. Ibid., p. 55.

# The Council-of-Governments Approach: Perceived Limitations and Problems

**5**

Councils of governments over the past twenty years have collectively and, in most instances, singularly demonstrated their utility and value. Councils have accomplished endeavors of a substantive, though perhaps, unspectacular nature. They have brought local officials of the metropolitan area into a meaningful dialogue for the purpose of discussing common and regional problems and for fashioning uniform policies to deal with these problems. Councils have engendered further horizontal cooperation between local governments and promoted vertical channels of access and communication between the local, state and national levels of governments. These bodies have been markedly successful in promoting the concept and interests of regionalism. Nevertheless, councils and the council approach continue to be plagued by several perceived limitations and areas of controversy, of both an immediate and long-term import, to which we now turn.

## Preference for
## Noncontroversial Activities

First, with the obvious and real exception of a limited number of councils—most notably the Association of Bay Area Governments (ABAG) and the Metropolitan Washington Council of Governments (COG)—these bodies have a marked tendency to engage in activities of a noncontroversial and systems-maintenance variety. Although the panorama, or scope of concern, of councils has widened, their heritage and organizational requirement of action based upon consensus usually prevents or precludes these bodies from responding in a substantive fashion to human and social problems found in the metropolis.

Victor Jones, affiliated with the University of California at Berkeley and a long-time observer and scholar of councils, more than a decade ago noted the often reluctant nature of councils to deal with substantive problems and the consequences that would result from this inaction:

> All existing metropolitan associations of local governments are so afraid of assuming responsibility for making decisions about a metropolitan problem—of appearing in the slightest to act as a "government"—that special districts will inevitably be proposed either by an association itself or by other forces in the metropolis to fill the governmental vacuum.[1]

Charles Harris, in his survey of councils of governments in 1969, assessed their involvement in the four broad social-program areas of housing, law enforcement, health and welfare, and education. Harris found that only twenty-four out of his sample of seventy-four councils, or about thirty-two percent, devoted a portion of the budget to these social areas;[2] where applicable this involved, on the average, approximately sixteen percent of the total council budget.[3] In addition, Harris found that fifty-five, or about seventy-five percent, of these bodies "had not established or did not indicate the establishment of special or standing committees in the social programs area."[4] Harris notes that, even in those instances where councils indicated they were involved in social problems, the nature of this involvement was often only of a superficial nature. He reminds the reader that although, for instance, approximately seventy percent of the councils included in the sample had devoted some measure of attention to the problem of housing, this figure was somewhat misleading because "the overwhelming majority of the COG's surveyed had not gone beyond the preliminary planning stage or discussion of the problem. Their discussions had dealt mainly with inventories, zoning and codes (standardization, uniformity of interpretation, etc.)."[5] Regarding council involvement in social problems, Harris concluded: "The charters, by-laws and other published documents of COGs emphasize the fact that these organizations will deal with regional problems of 'mutual concern' to the members' jurisdictions. To date the record does not show very much concern about social problems."[6]

In general, it is reasonable to assume that the executive directors and staffs of councils of governments would prefer to see their organizations more directly involved in alleviating the social problems of their area, but this involvement is usually frustrated by the mandate of councils to only engage in activity of a consensual nature. Declared the former executive director of a now defunct council: "I would like the Conference to become more involved in controversial items . . . it might even be good for the organization . . . but the members . . . well, they wish the Conference to refrain from doing so."[7] The early attempt, in its formative years, of the Capitol Region Council of Elected Officials (CRCEO) to examine and develop a regional approach regarding the problem of housing in the

Hartford, Connecticut, area almost proved fatal to the organization. The then chairman of CRCEO related:

> No, I didn't think it was a good idea to bring Brown's [James Brown, of the metropolitan planning agency] proposal [on housing] before the members of the council. I knew it would be too controversial. You know, I waited in apprehension until the next meeting to see how many members would show up. Fortunately, most of them did show up the next time.[8]

As elaborated upon in the preceding chapter, councils of governments have become involved with such human-oriented concerns as employment, housing, health, and law enforcement. But this involvement, to a major extent encouraged and mandated by the federal government, tends to be primarily of a planning nature, rather than involving program implementation. It is reasonable to assume that, until councils generally become more decidedly involved in alleviating human and social problems, many observers of the urban scene will continue to dismiss their usefulness and value and continue to urge the necessity of some version of comprehensive metropolitan government as a requisite first step to be taken in order that we may more effectively deal with our urban problems.

### Limited Representative Commitment and Involvement

Second, another problem confronting councils of governments has been the usually limited nature of the commitment, identification, and involvement of council representatives. Regarding this, Royce Hanson has written:

> A basic problem of the councils . . . is reflected in the limited interests, power, and time of its participants, all or most of whom are elected officials with primary political loyalty to and duties in their own jurisdications. . . . The council competes with a myriad of other organizations, great and small, for the time and interest of its members.[9]

Joseph F. Zimmerman has noted: "In most cases, the number of elected officials active in a metropolitan council tends to be relatively small, and the average official who attends the annual meeting of the council will not identify himself closely with it."[10] In a very real sense, relatively few council representatives devote much of their time to council activities and programs, and hence their involvement is of a minimal nature. As a result, Harris notes: "Interviews with elected officials serving on councils of governments revealed that many of them had abdicated their leadership responsibilities, leaving things more or less to the executive staff."[11] Somewhat reflective of the general low level of the representatives in councils, Dana Hansen, who served in a supporting liaison role between the Greater Hartford Chamber of Commerce and the Capitol Region Council of Elected Officials (CRCEO), noted:

> Sure, Aston [the Chairman] and I did most of the work. We made the decisions. Now the reason why Aston was so involved is because he is really interested in regional problems. There is no doubt about that. And he wanted to make something of the council. Now, why am I so involved? Because it is my business, it is my job.

Hansen went on to state:

> Yes, we had committees. When some sort of issue came up, we would create a committee to look into it. But they really were not real committees. Aston and I would do the real job of looking into the problem.[12]

The often limited involvement of representatives in council activities and deliberations is somewhat accounted for by the fact that these individuals usually have other personal and public responsibilities that demand much of their time. One representative, queried as to why he did not attend the initial meetings of the Capitol Region Council of Elected Officials (CRCEO) on a more regular basis, asserted:

> I did not attend the first two meetings of the council because
> of business around town. Why, the town budget was coming
> up and I had to prepare for that. That was more important
> to do than to attend the meetings of the council. Anyway, I
> plan to attend the next meeting. . . . I think I will be able
> to get away from here.[13]

In a somewhat similar vein, a fellow representative declared:

> I've attended one meeting of the three that the council has
> held. You know I have a business here in town, and I am
> mayor. Between tending to my business and being mayor, I
> am kept pretty busy.[14]

The irregular attendance behavior of many council representatives elicited this observation by the former executive director of the Regional Conference of Elected Officials (RCEO):

> You know it is quite difficult to get all of the elected officials
> to come to a meeting. . . . They have so many other things
> they are doing. They are not only elected officials but they
> are also, perhaps, businessmen. . . . Now with the techni-
> cal people [fire and police officials, etc.], there is no problem
> there. I can call an all-day meeting and they will all show up.
> But the elected officials feel they cannot take the entire day
> off; . . . they have so many things they have to do.[15]

To be sure, it is a structural inherent attribute of councils of governments that its participants will function in a part-time capacity since these representatives are usually chief elected officials, with competing municipal duties and responsibilities. This is not to suggest that being a representative, directly elected, to a council body should be the sole political function of an individual; after all, this would do violence with one of the basic characteristics of councils, since they are designed to be arenas where *local* elected officials can converse about and fashion uniform policies for regional problems. It seems clear, however, that until a larger segment of council representatives show a greater identification with, and commitment to, and

expend a larger portion of their time in council activities—
like the representatives involved in the Metropolitan
Washington Council of Governments[16]—the seemingly
low-level input of many council representatives will remain
an important hindrance to council development and involvement in alleviating urban problems.

## Representation
## and Voting Apportionment

Third, as empirical evidence gathered by the Advisory Commission on Intergovernmental Relations
(ACIR) and the International City Management Association documents (ICMA), issues relating to member representation and voting apportionment, at both the general-
assembly and executive board levels, have been among the
most serious and somewhat persistent problems confronted
by councils of governments.[17] Specifically, many councils
have had to contend with the issue of whether member
representation and voting apportionment should reflect the
traditional council formula of equal representation for
each governmental member ("one government-one vote"),
or whether council representation and voting apportionment should mirror, to some degree, the aggregate
population of each member. On the whole, the elected
officials of core cities believe, as self-interest and political
considerations would dictate, that council representation,
especially at the executive board level, should reflect to a
more marked degree the total population of each member
than is presently the case of most councils.[18] The demand
on the part of core-city officials that councils extend
greater consideration to the aggregate population of each
member when devising representation and voting apportionment formulas is somewhat legitimatized and supported by the findings of Harris, who noted that a plural-
ity, about forty-five percent, of the council executive

directors he surveyed were of the persuasion that "suburban areas [are] overrepresented from [a] population standpoint in council deliberations."[19] On the other hand, suburban officials, fearful of core-city domination of council activities and the council decision-making process generally, oppose any council representation and voting formulas based exclusively or almost entirely on population criteria. Although somewhat muted, the traditional suburban mistrust and suspicion of core cities has not been isolated from the council-of-governments experience. For instance, Wyn N. Hoadley in her study of the East-West Gateway Coordinating Council, of the St. Louis area, found that many of the suburban assembly representatives are of the opinion that smaller municipalities are not given adequate representation on the executive board, and they perceived the mayor of St. Louis as clearly the dominant personality in council deliberations.[20] We should note that the supposed domination by New York City of the Metropolitan Regional Council in the late fifties, at least as perceived by suburban officials, led to a period of organizational instability.[21]

Many councils of governments, in response to core-city dissatisfaction of the standard council representation and voting formula of "one government, one vote," have adopted more flexible formulas relative to representation and voting privileges. As noted earlier in this work, about one-half of the councils have representation formulas for both the general assembly and executive board levels that give some consideration to the total population of each member. Harris found that councils generally tend to enhance core-city representation at the executive board level.[22] Although some councils of governments are still plagued by issues relating to representation and voting apportionment, most municipal and county officials are reasonably satisfied with the nature of their jurisdictional representation on council bodies.[23] The U.S. District Court in Connecticut has ruled that the doctrine of "one man, one vote" as laid down in the Supreme Court decision of *Reynolds* v. *Sims*[24] does not apply to councils because, strictly speaking, they are not governmental bodies nor do they perform governmental functions *per se.*[25] However, if council bodies evolve into limited metropolitan governments, the problem of representation could again become manifest in view of the United States Supreme Court decisions of *Avery* v. *Midland County*[26] and *Hadley* v. *The Junior College District of Kansas City,*[27] that applied the "one man, one vote" dictum to local government.

## Dependence on
## Federal Fiscal Resources

Fourth, another area of concern regarding councils of governments involves their pattern of financing and sources of revenues. As noted previously, councils enjoy the indigenous financial support of their members through the employment of membership dues and other forms of financial assessments. However, in practically all instances, revenues internally generated account for only a small share of any one council's financial resources. For instance, in fiscal year 1975 the Metropolitan Washington Council of Governments (COG) derived only about fourteen percent of its financial resources from member units.[28] One study found that, in the 1971 fiscal year, fifty-one percent of the regional councils secured no more than thirty percent of their financial support from their members.[29] Likewise, state funding for councils of governments has been generally of a minimal or token level; in the 1971 fiscal year, approximately seventy-two percent of the councils obtained only thirty percent or less of their financial assistance from the state level.[30]

As the preceding discussion implies, councils of governments have been overly dependent on federal financial assistance, especially in the form of "701" comprehensive planning grants. For instance, in fiscal year 1971, fifty-six percent of the councils secured sixty-one percent or more of their total revenues via federal funding.[31] Melvin Mogulof has noted: "It is Federal money, Federal staff assistance and Federal policy that is largely responsible for the health and/or weakness of the COG."[32] The inordinate reliance of councils of governments on federal grants of one variety or another has incurred several negative costs on these bodies. First, it has obviously encouraged council activity in those areas where federal monetary assistance is available and tended to discourage council involvement in those problem areas where federal assistance is absent; I am suggesting that federal grants have played a disproportionate role in structuring council agenda and programmatic activities, to some degree, at the expense of council noninvolvement in the more critical problems found in the various metropolitan regions. And second, the dependence of councils of governments on federal annual grant assistance has served to retard their ability to develop, plan, and implement long-term programs and activities. In order to be more relevant and responsive organizations, councils must become less dependent on federal grants by securing expanded local and state sources of financial support. In the future, we should expect that the primary sources of increased revenues for councils of governments will be derived from these two levels of government.

## Relationship with
## Other Governmental Entities

Fifth, another subject of concern involves the institutional and programmatic relationship of councils of governments with special districts and authorities and with other area-wide planning organizations found in the metropolis. The manner in which councils should interface and interact with these governmental bodies has been the focus of considerable debate. Council monitoring and review of the activities of authorities and special districts is hampered because generally these bodies are not members of councils; specifically, only about ten percent of the council organizations, such as the Southeast Michigan Council of Governments (SEMCOG), allow special districts to partake in membership.[33]

Over the past decade, various components of the federal government, most especially the Departments of Housing and Urban Development, Transportation, Health, Education, and Welfare, and the Environmental Protection Agency, have sponsored the creation and proliferation of numerous uni-functional area-wide planning bodies, involving such matters as health, transportation, economic development, and law enforcement.[34] In general, this development has had a negative effect in several ways on councils of governments. First, the existence of segmental area-wide planning organizations in the metropolis has, to some extent, deprived councils from becoming more involved in salient social and human problems; and, second, these bodies have often proved to be in competition with councils for local political and fiscal support. In one instance, the proliferation of uni-functional area-wide planning bodies was obliquely partly responsible for the eventual demise of a council.[35] As the Advisory Commission on Intergovernmental Relations (ACIR) noted:

> With the growth of regionalism came rising expectations for regional action, but there also is growing competition among the various regional organizations and a nagging confusion spawned by Federal program complexities and inconsistencies.[36]

The introduction of uni-functional area-wide planning bodies in the metropolis, organizationally independent of councils of governments, has further confused the pattern of area-wide planning and decision-making. As one study well summarizes:

> Thus, the success that Federal agencies have in encouraging new regions, and in building new area-wide organizations for their own program purposes, tends more toward increasing the complexity of government than toward providing a single comprehensive mechanism at the regional level.[37]

It seems clear that, if councils of governments are going to maximize their role of being comprehensive metropolitan planning, program, and policy coordinators, several recommendations are in order. First, all councils should allow authorities and special districts to be members of and partake in council activities. This is only reasonable given the increasing number of authorities and special districts found in the metropolis, and their central role in providing to the public a wide range of services. Further, allowing special districts and authorities to partake in council deliberations and activities would serve to broaden the membership base of councils and enhance their representative quality. And, second, to facilitate greater comprehensiveness and integration in regional planning, the responsibilities and activities of unifunctional planning agencies should be transferred to councils of governments.

## Councils and the Black Community

Sixth, a matter of considerable debate focuses on the present and future relationship of councils of governments with the black community. As population statistics and trends well document, blacks are becoming increasingly numerous in core cities; indeed, in Washington, D.C., Atlanta, Newark, and Gary, Indiana, to cite several examples, blacks constitute a majority of the population. Through the employment of mobilizing present and future black majorities, some black political leaders endeavor to enhance black political development and strength and to gain political control of core cities.[38]

According to one body of thought, black political leaders believe they are on the verge of capturing political control of core cities and hence they view in askance metropolitan political consolidation and policies generally designed to further political metropolitanism.[39] Metropolitan government with a usual consequent majority of white voters, according to this point of view, would serve to dilute black political strength and retard black political development, and therefore should be opposed. Black skepticism of consolidated metropolitan government has been reflected in black electoral behavior on metropolitan political reform proposals. As Dale Rogers Marshall has written: "A majority of blacks typically oppose metropolitan proposals as shown in the literature on the politics of reform. The studies of Cleveland, St. Louis, Miami, and Nashville all show Negroes voting against metropolitan reform proposals."[40] According to Marshall, the general negative attitude that blacks harbor toward consolidated metropolitan government makes them oppose incremental reforms as well, such as exemplified by councils of governments:

> To summarize, the limited evidence on the attitudes of minority leaders and voters toward metropolitan radical reform proposals, existing metropolitan governments, and *proposed incremental reforms* (italics mine) indicates opposition to metropolitan government of any type.[41]

Francis Fox Piven and Richard A. Cloward commenting, in several articles published in *The New Republic* in 1967, on federal policies designed to spur councils of governments and regionalism expressed agreement with those blacks who view incremental metropolitan reform as being injurious to their political position. Piven and Cloward wrote: "The autonomy of local government will not be the only casualty of administrative metropolitanism; Negroes will be the losers too."[42]

On the other hand, empirical evidence does not support the contention that black political leaders are united in their opposition to councils of governments; rather, black political leaders appear to be noticeably divided in their attitudes toward councils. Some black leaders view councils as mechanisms that will ensure black participation in regional decision-making and as vehicles that can play a significant role in alleviating the social problems of core cities. Black political leaders, such as Thomas Bradley[43] of Los Angeles, Richard Austin of Detroit, and Walter Washington of the District of Columbia, have been especially active in their respective councils of governments. In 1972, the Joint Center for Political Studies, in a survey of black elected officials, found that fifty-eight percent of the respondents were of the persuasion that regional councils would or could help blacks of the core cities deal with their problems, while thirty-seven percent were convinced that councils were or could be a clear threat to black interests; five percent felt that councils had no direct positive or negative bearing on the black community.[44]

What accounts for the divided attitude of black political leaders toward councils of governments? To some extent the individual perceptions of black political leaders of councils are derived from what each perceives to be in the best interest of the black community; on the other hand, some individual black attitudes toward councils are the product of perceived self-interest. Piven and Cloward remind us that some professional blacks stand to gain from metropolitan political regionalism.[45] Harris asserts that the individual attitudes of black political leaders toward councils is to some degree shaped by whether or not they have been involved in council activities:

118

Black leaders officially connected with the COG of their region and knowledgeable about its program were formally inclined toward it. Those not connected with but knowledgeable about the COG and its operation generally were not favorably disposed toward it and were much less optimistic about its potential for contributing to the solution of critical urban problems. The sharpest opposition came from those leaders who focused solely or primarily on the political-elective aspects of the regional movement, and did not consider the broader pros and cons of the urban problem complex and how those problems might be resolved or not resolved over the long haul.[46]

In order to be perceived as legitimate and viable organizations, councils of governments must cultivate and gain broad support in the black community. It is clear that councils need to increase the number of blacks on their staffs and policy boards. As one study notes: "Generally, local black elected officials have been unsatisfied with black representation on policy boards and staffs of regional councils, particularly the latter."[47] And second, councils need to be more directly involved in alleviating the social problems of the black community. Although black political leaders generally accord high praise for the physical planning activities of councils, they have generally discounted the effectiveness of council involvement in social problems.[48] Council of governments involvement in social problems is crucial for as Harris notes: "To the extent that COGs cannot deal effectively with social problems, they cannot respond to the needs of the blacks and the poor."[49]

## Lack of Saliency and Citizen Involvement

Seventh, the effectiveness and utility of councils of governments has been somewhat curtailed by their relative lack of public saliency and low levels of citizen involvement and input. In terms of public familiarity, councils in smaller population areas have faired somewhat

119

better than their counterparts in larger areas.[50] Generating adequate and relevant citizen participation, especially from the poor and minorities, in activities and decision-making has been a major problem for councils. Mogulof has noted: "It is apparent that the overwhelming number of citizen members on COG boards would be better described as white and middle class rather than being of a visible minority."[51] Harris found that only nine of the seventy-four executive directors of councils he queried believe the general public enjoyed an "excellent" or "good" awareness of council activities, while fifty-six of the directors acknowledged that public awareness of their council's activities was of only a "fair" or "poor" level.[52] The general ignorance of councils is exemplified by the following reply of a local political party chairman who when asked to comment upon the nascent Capitol Region Council of Elected Officials (CRCEO) in the Hartford, Connecticut, area stated:

> What council? I have never heard of CRCEO. When did all this come about? It sounds good . . . but I never knew there was such a thing. . . . No one else in the town has heard of it either.[53]

Similarly, another local party chairman exclaimed:

> CRCEO . . . what is that? You mean the Planning Agency [Capitol Regional Planning Agency]? . . . I don't know anything about the council.[54]

Public ignorance of and indifference toward councils of governments may be partly attributed to several factors. As numerous studies have substantiated, many Americans are politically apathetic and exhibit very little real continuous interest in politics.[55] And second, the indirect nature of council representation, where representatives serve in an *ex-officio* capacity, and the limited and narrow functional concerns of councils mitigate against citizen awareness of these bodies.

Councils of governments, in the quest of gaining more

public saliency and ensuring greater citizen input, have resorted to a number of strategies and techniques. Practically all councils distribute, usually on a monthly basis, an information newsletter to their membership and other interested groups and individuals. The staff of councils speak on council undertakings and other topics before community and regional groups and over the mass media; the latter is one of the most effective means of informing the public about council activities.[56] In addition, many councils have established citizen advisory committees facilitating broader public input into council policy-making. For instance, the Metropolitan Washington Council of Governments (COG) has created citizen advisory committees whose areas of concern involve either land use, human resources, public safety, health, environmental protection, or transportation.[57] Finally, some councils have adopted the practice of conducting public hearings on problems confronting their region. Undoubtedly, these measures will increase citizen awareness of councils and enhance their public standing.

## End Itself
## or Strategy of Reform?

A final matter of discussion, of a broader and philosophical import, regarding the council-of-governments approach, is whether councils should be ascertained as ends themselves or as transitory structures central to a strategy of reform designed to bring about some variant of comprehensive metropolitan government. It appears that supporters of the council concept may be, for the sake of analysis, divided into two broad groupings. One category is composed of a clear majority of local elected public officials who view the council as a worthwhile institution *per se,* but who are adverse to granting substantive powers or responsibilities to these bodies; certainly, as I have written elsewhere, a vast majority of those interviewed by the author in Connecticut are of this persuasion:

> Substantial support for a limited regional council was evident among those interviewed. While 85 percent accept the need for a council in their region, 74 percent felt it should be purely advisory. Except for the managers in the cities and towns, a council with substantive powers is contraindicative.[58]

In a similar, but in a more comparative sense, G. Ross Stephens of the University of Missouri-Kansas City has written:

> Given federal, and in some cases state, support for the formation of COGs, local officials are willing to go along with voluntary associations of local governments. They are currently unwilling to give "power" to those agencies or pursue the creation of anything resembling a metropolitan government. Local officials will not voluntarily countenance anything that disturbs the *status quo* and the traditions of local self-rule.[59]

On the other hand, there are those advocates of councils, albeit a minority of local officials, who support councils, not so much because they are convinced about utility and resourcefulness of these bodies, but rather because they perceive councils as mechanisms through which the goal of consolidated metropolitan government might be realized. In a very real sense, these supporters, whether federal, state, or local officials, or council staff members, view councils as fundamental blocks in the building and legitimatizing of institutional metropolitanism. (Melvin Mogulof has written: "There are those in the federal government who do view the COG developmentally."[60]) Local officials who are in this grouping tend to be more active and involved in council affairs than most of their colleagues. For instance, Hoadley in her study of the attitudes of the representatives involved in the East-West Coordinating Council, of the St. Louis area, found that council officers were more receptive to an institutionally strengthened organization than nonoffice holders:

> Very few members felt that the council's powers should be decreased. *Board members tended to favor an increase in powers* while the regular members regarded the present setup as satisfactory. On the whole the *granting of taxing power was not favored although, again, board members were more sympathetic* toward the suggestion than the regular members (italics mine).[61]

Similarly, Thomas Cronin notes that the members of the Executive Committee of the Association of Bay Area Governments (ABAG) generally are more regionally oriented and indicate a greater preference for transforming ABAG into a limited metropolitan government than the rest of the delegates.[62] In summary, one can speculate that those representatives who take a more active and involved role in councils over a period of time develop a rather pronounced regional perspective.

Whether councils of governments should be viewed as ends in themselves or as simply crucial elements in bringing about metropolitan structural political reform is, of course, a normative question. This issue, however, does render it somewhat more difficult to arrive at some universal conclusions about the value and utility of the council device.

## Conclusions

This chapter has cited and elaborated upon some of the problems and perceived limitations of councils of governments. To be sure, these problems and limitations have somewhat curtailed the effectiveness and utility of councils in confronting and developing policies and programs for alleviating economic and social problems found in the metropolis. However, what should be recognized is that notwithstanding these problems and limitations—which most councils through adopting appropriate structural and other changes are rendering less severe—the assorted achievements and accomplishments of councils of governments are considerable.

# Notes

1. Victor Jones, "Cooperative Pattern," *National Civic Review* 51 (June 1962): 304.
2. Charles Harris, *Regional COG's and the Central City* (Detroit: Metropolitan Fund, 1970), p. 14.
3. Ibid.
4. Ibid., p. 15.
5. Charles Harris, "Blacks and Regionalism: Councils of Governments," *National Civic Review* 62 (May 1973): 257.
6. Ibid.
7. Interview with Chester A. Kunz, Executive Director of the Regional Conference of Elected Officials (RCEO), June 6, 1967.
8. Interview with Walter Aston, Chairman, Capitol Region Council of Elected Officials, August 10, 1967.
9. Royce Hanson, *Metropolitan Councils of Governments* (Washington, D.C.: Advisory Commission on Intergovernmental Relations, 1966), p. 34.
10. Joseph F. Zimmerman, "Metropolitan Ecumenism: The Road to the Promised Land?" *Journal of Urban Law* 44 (Spring 1967): 452.
11. Harris, *Regional COG's and the Central City,* p. 23.
12. Interview with Dana Hansen, Manager of Regional Development, Greater Hartford Chamber of Commerce, August 8, 1967.
13. Interview with Norman I. Adams, First Selectman, East Granby, Conn., September 14, 1966.
14. Interview with Thomas J. McCusker, Mayor, Vernon, Conn., July 19, 1966.
15. Kunz interview, June 6, 1967.
16. Walter Scheiber, Executive Director of the Metropolitan Washington Council of Governments (COG), to some degree credits the general sophistication and high level of educational attainment of the inhabitants of the Washington, D.C. area for the extent of representative involvement in the council; gained in interview, November 27, 1974.

17. Advisory Commission on Intergovernmental Relations, *Regional Decision Making: New Strategies for Substate Districts* (Washington, D.C.: The Commission, 1973), p. 103.
18. Indeed, the City of Milwaukee has refused to join the Intergovernmental Cooperation Council for Milwaukee County because of the refusal of the Council to grant Milwaukee voting privileges somewhat reflective of its total population. See Henry W. Maier, "Conflict in Metropolitan Areas," *The Annals of the American Academy of Political and Social Science* 416 (November 1974): 156.
19. Harris, *Regional COG's and the Central City,* p. 6.
20. Wyn N. Hoadley, "Metropolitan Councils: The St. Louis Experience," *National Civic Review* 60 (February 1971): 83.
21. Advisory Commission on Intergovernmental Relations, *Regional Decision Making,* p. 64; for an excellent work on the Metropolitan Regional Council, see Joan B. Aron, *The Quest for Regional Cooperation: A Study of the New York Metropolitan Regional Council* (Berkeley: University of California Press, 1969).
22. Harris, *Regional COG's and the Central City,* pp. 6-7.
23. Advisory Commission on Intergovernmental Relations, *Regional Decision Making,* p. 119.
24. Reynolds v. Sims, 377 U.S. 533 (1964).
25. Education/Instruction et al. v. Thomas Moore, Chairman of the Capitol Regional Planning Agency, Hartford, Connecticut, et al. (1973), cited in Jean Gansel, "Regional Council Directors: Perspectives of External Influence," in *The Municipal Yearbook, 1973* (Washington, D.C.: International City Management Association, 1973), p. 54.
26. Avery v. Midland County, 390 U.S. 474 (1968).
27. Hadley v. The Junior College District of Kansas City, 397 U.S. 50 (1970).
28. Metropolitan Washington Council of Governments, *Goals, Objectives, and Work Program: for Greater Washington,* (Washington, D.C.: The Council, 1974), p. 21.
29. Advisory Commission on Intergovernmental Relations, *Regional Decision Making,* p. 89.
30. Ibid.
31. Ibid.
32. Melvin B. Mogulof, *Governing Metropolitan Areas: A Critical Review of Councils of Governments and the Federal Role* (Washington, D.C.: The Urban Institute, 1971), p. 13.

33. National Service to Regional Councils, *Regionalism: A New Dimension in Local Government and Intergovernmental Relations* (Washington, D.C.: The Service, 1971), p. 14.

34. See Chapter VI, "Federal Programs Supporting Substate Regionalism," in Advisory Commission on Intergovernmental Relations, *Regional Decision Making*, 167-220.

35. The proliferation of uni-functional planning agencies and other regional governmental entities in the Atlanta area partially accounted for the demise of the Metropolitan Atlanta Council of Local Governments (MACLOG) and the emergence of the Atlanta Regional Commission in 1971. Gained in interview with Harry West, Executive Director, Atlanta Regional Commission, November 6, 1974.

36. Advisory Commission on Intergovernmental Relations, *Regional Decision Making*, p. 197.

37. Ibid., p. 202.

38. For two excellent essays on the relationship of metropolitan government and the black community, see Tobe Johnson, *Metropolitan Government: A Black Analytical Perspective* (Washington, D.C.: Joint Center for Political Studies, 1972), and, Dale Rogers Marshall, "Metropolitan Government: Views of Minorities," in *Minority Perspectives*, ed. Lowdon Wingo (Washington, D.C.: Resources for the Future, 1972), pp. 9-30.

39. Marshall, "Metropolitan Government," pp. 20-21.

40. Ibid., p. 15.

41. Ibid., p. 20.

42. Frances Fox Piven and Richard A. Cloward, "Black Control of Cities: Heading Off by Metropolitan Government," *New Republic*, 30 September 1967, pp. 19-20.

43. Thomas Bradley, "Regional Governance and Racial and Ethnic Minorities," in *The Regionalist Papers*, ed. Kent Mathewson (Detroit: Metropolitan Fund, 1974), pp. 163-173.

44. Advisory Commission on Intergovernmental Relations, *Regional Decision Making*, p. 137.

45. Frances Fox Piven and Richard A. Cloward, "Black Control of Cities—II: How the Negroes Will Lose," *New Republic*, 7 October 1967, p. 15.

46. Harris, "Blacks and Regionalism," p. 255.

47. Advisory Commission on Intergovernmental Relations, *Regional Decision Making*, p. 134.

48. Ibid.
49. Harris, "Blacks and Regionalism," p. 258.
50. Harris, *Regional COG's and the Central City*, p. 19.
51. Mogulof, *Governing Metropolitan Areas*, p. 84.
52. Harris, *Regional COG's and the Central City*, p. 19.
53. Interview with Gordon F. Granger, Republican Town Chairman, East Granby, Conn., September 16, 1966.
54. Interview with Robert Noonan, Democratic Town Chairman, Tolland, Conn., August 19, 1966.
55. See, for example, Lester Milbrath, *Political Participation* (Chicago: Rand McNally, 1965), pp. 16-18.
56. Gansel, "Regional Council Directors," p. 50.
57. Metropolitan Washington Council of Governments, *Goals, Objectives, and Work Program*, p. 28.
58. Nelson Wikstrom, "Attitudes Toward COGs in Connecticut," *Midwest Review of Public Administration* 5 (February 1971): 43.
59. G. Ross Stephens, "Some Concluding Observations," *Midwest Review of Public Administration* 5 (February 1971): 47-48.
60. Mogulof, *Governing Metropolitan Areas*, p. 19.
61. Hoadley, "Metropolitan Councils," p. 81.
62. Frederick M. Wirt, *Power in the City: Decision Making in San Francisco* (Berkeley: University of California Press, 1974), p. 315.

# Councils of Governments and the Metropolitan World 6

Councils of governments are, in a sense, a product of the times. The rapid expansion and growth of suburbia, encouraged and stimulated by federal governmental policies, particularly in the area of housing, expressways and highways, and urban renewal, obliquely is responsible for the proliferation of councils. As the spread of metropolitan areas became larger in scope commencing in the late forties, it soon became apparent that at least some matters, such as overall land use, air and water pollution, and highways and mass transportation, had to be examined and approached from a regional perspective. In order to facilitate this perspective some sort of *politically acceptable* regional structure is necessary; a council of governments conveniently meets this need.

As elaborated upon previously in this work, councils of governments have come into being because a majority of local officials are supportive of these bodies and assorted federal policies have encouraged or mandated their formation; some states, as well, have stimulated through various ways the establishment of councils. Local officials support councils for they perceive a need for such an organization where they can converse about mutual problems and develop and negotiate regional policies. One of the most important political developments in our federal system over the last fifteen years has been the decided involvement of the federal government in our urban areas. The desire of the federal government to build at least some measure of formal rudimentary metropolitan political structure has resulted in the rise and establishment of councils of governments.

## Achievements of
## Councils of Governments

The achievements of councils of governments are considerable. Councils have served as vehicles of incremental political change, both of a structural and an attitudinal nature. Councils have provided a *neutral* arena or forum where like elected officials can familiarize themselves with each other and discuss mutual and regional problems, and policies to be adopted to alleviate these problems. These bodies have served to mediate core-city and suburban conflict and distrust. In their role as A-95 federal review agencies and through their planning endeavors, councils have facilitated specific functional and comprehensive regional planning. Councils of governments have brought about not only greater horizontal intergovernmental cooperation, but also governmental cooperation of a vertical nature, i.e., between local, state, and federal bodies. As a result of their institutionalization in the American polity, councils of governments have emerged as the "fourth component or layer" in our system of federalism.

Each of the above are creditable achievements of the council-of-governments approach. However, the most significant contribution of councils is that they have furthered the concept and interests of regionalism. Reflective of this, the sort of metropolitan leadership and regional statesmanship that was so lacking in American urban areas two decades ago is now developing and visible, thanks in large part to the council movement. Local officials identify more strongly than ever before with their respective council organizations.

Melvin B. Mogulof has noted in his work, *Governing Metropolitan Areas: A Critical Review of Councils of Governments and the Federal Role,* the key function that councils have played in promoting regionalism:

> Every COG we have observed has helped to create a sense of regional community. Interdependencies have been sharpened and an institution has been created which continuously poses expectations for regional action. The COG has had some small successes in an area of American governance where there has been very little public willingness to recognize the existence of problems.[1]

Further, Mogulof penned:

> The presence of a COG-type mechanism in almost all of our metropolitan areas is precisely the reason why there is new hope and excitement on the metropolitan governing scene. COGs have helped to congeal a metropolitan community and to create a metropolitan point of view. COGs have assembled staff able to see solutions to problems across jurisdictional lines and they have given a platform to regional leadership. COGs have acted as a spur to state involvement in the region, and they have punctured the isolationism of single purpose agencies. We find the COG to be a mechanism worthy of (and reflective of) the intelligence invested in it by the OMB, HUD, local government officials and COG staff.[2]

The success that councils have had in promoting and institutionalizing regionalism in metropolitan areas has had several effects. First, in several urban areas serious consideration has been given to, or there has actually emerged, regional political structures incrementally stronger (i.e., vested with powers of one variety or other) than a council. On several occasions the Association of Bay Area Governments (ABAG) was nearly transformed, by appropriate state legislation, into a limited metropolitan government for the San Francisco area. The activities and functions of the Metropolitan Atlanta Council of Local Governments (MACLOG), along with several other regional entities, became the responsibility of the Atlanta Regional Commission (ARC) when it was formed in 1971. Unlike as in the case with councils of governments, local governments in the Atlanta Standard Metropolitan Statistical Area are required to belong to and contribute financial support to the ARC.[3] And second, the Advisory Commission on Intergovernmental Relations (ACIR), discerning the increasing credence of regionalism, has recommended the establishment in each metropolitan area of an "umbrella multijurisdictional organization" to carry on council activities and functions.[4] As in the instance of the Atlanta Regional Commission and the Metropolitan Council of Minneapolis-St. Paul,[5] local government membership and financial support for these bodies would be mandatory. These developments strongly suggest that councils of governments should be evaluated from both a developmental as well as institutional point of view.

### A Developmental Typology of Councils

Chart 4 presents in a schematic fashion a developmental typology of councils of governments, based on and derived from information gathered for this study. The basic features of this developmental typology are as follows. First, each council is established because of essentially the same reasons (reasons which have been cited and elaborated upon previously in this volume). Second, once established all councils can *potentially* follow a similar

## CHART 4

### A DEVELOPMENTAL TYPOLOGY FOR COUNCILS OF GOVERNMENTS: SCHEMATIC DESIGN

| CHARACTERISTICS | INITIAL | CONSOLIDATION | INSTITUTIONALIZED |
|---|---|---|---|
| Key attributes | Advisory and voluntary | Advisory and voluntary | Limited powers, quasi-mandatory membership |
| Organizational structure | Weakly articulated | Somewhat articulated | Well articulated |
| Local government participation | Substantial | Greater participation | Near-universal participation |
| Staff | Extremely limited | Limited | Extensive |
| Budget | Extremely limited | Limited | Extensive |
| Delegate identification | Weak | Moderately weak | Moderately strong |
| Nature of activities | Non-controversial | Non-controversial | Largely noncontroversial, some of a controversial nature |
| Decision-making | Consensual | Consensual | Majority-minority oriented |

course of development passing through two distinct stages, or phases, of development — "initial" and "consolidation"—before emerging as an "institutionalized" council. This typology is of an indeterminate quality for it acknowledges that not all councils emerge as "institutionalized" bodies. Further, by the term *consolidationist*, I am simply making reference to a council whose continued existence is no longer in doubt; an "institutionalized" council is one that enjoys a *modest* amount of power and influence in the metropolitan region.

And finally, this typology of councils sets forth the key characteristics of each stage of council development. While most of these characteristics are readily understandable, several are not. For instance, by the term *weakly articulated* organizational structure, I am simply acknowledging that during the "initial" period of council development the organizational structure of councils, especially in terms of committee structure, is not clearly defined or fixed. Further, by the term *majority-minority* oriented decision-making, I am suggesting that "institutionalized" councils appear more willing to decide council issues and policies on the basis of simply a majority vote, rather than attempting to develop a universal consensus. Finally, by the term *quasi-mandatory membership,* identified as a key characteristic of an "institutionalized" council, I am asserting that, although a local government is not *formally* mandated to be a member of a council, it is decidedly in its interest to partake in council membership.

## A Refutation of
## Metropolitan Government

Any defense of the council-of-governments approach requires by implication at least some modest evidence that consolidated metropolitan governmental reform is not preferable or needed; what immediately follows, then, is material supportive of this position. First, one compelling argument against metropolitan government relates to citizen or democratic preference. Clearly, as popular referenda and survey data substantiate, the vast majority of the citizenry residing in our large urban areas oppose metropolitan government. Blacks, dwelling largely in core cities, fear that metropolitan government would prove to be inimical to their political interests and position.[6] Robert Wood has detailed in length how the "typical" suburbanite perceives her or his community to be a "miniature republic" and views with alarm any action that would serve to reduce its political autonomy.[7] In summary, the service priorities and political interests of individuals cause most of them to oppose metropolitan governmental reform proposals.

Second, empirical evidence does not necessarily support the several contentions of the "consolidationists" that governmental organization in the metropolis is chaotic and that the per capita costs of local governmental services, due to the lack of a unified regional approach, are higher than they need be. Studies indicate that, by the process of what Charles Lindblom has called "coordination through mutual adjustment,"[8] there is far more cooperation between governments in the metropolis than we have commonly believed or acknowledged. Vincent Ostrom, Charles Tiebout, and Robert Warren certainly found this to be the case in the Los Angeles area at the beginning of the sixties.[9] Similarly, H. Paul Friesema discovered a rather elaborate system of cooperation between local governments in the Quad-City metropolitan area of Illinois and Iowa.[10] In a more general sense, Joseph F. Zimmerman, as earlier noted, has documented the extensive number and variety of contractual agreements between local governments. Given the above and other evidence, it is simply not accurate to portray the governmental organization of the metropolis as chaotic and composed of *isolated* political units.

Further, numerous studies do not support the notion that the fragmented nature of urban government serves to enhance the per capita costs of local public services. As previously noted, Brett Hawkins and Thomas Dye found no relationship between the extent of fragmented urban government and the costs or quality of municipal services.[11] Similarly, in their inquiry, Alan Campbell and Seymour Sacks discerned no *consistent* relationship between measures of governmental fragmentation and per capita municipal expenditures.[12]

In addition, some scholars have begun to question the once widely held belief that metropolitan government, by taking advantage of the economies of scale, can lower the per capita costs of local public services. As long ago as 1967, Robert Dahl asserted:

> There is, for example, no worthwhile evidence that there are any significant economies of scale in city governments for cities over about 50,000. The few items on which increasing size does lead to decreasing unit costs, such as water and sewerage, are too small a proposition of total city outlays to lead to significant economies; and, even these reductions are probably offset by rising costs for other services, such as police protection.[13]

After a summary review of the literature on city size and percapita expenditures, Robert L. Bish and Vincent Ostrom concluded: "Such data clearly do *not* support the contention that an increase in organizational size associated with consolidation will reduce costs."[14] Indeed, several studies have found that the per capita costs of public services increases, rather than declines, with the establishment of metropolitan government.

Third, advocates of metropolitan government have argued that only by establishing such structures can one effectively counteract the disparity of fiscal resources available to municipalities and ensure equality of service levels throughout the metropolitan area. Yet, as Robert Bish reminds us, individuals dwelling in urban areas often entertain differing public service priorities; for example, as Bish notes: "Some individuals prefer to use their economic resources to obtain larger private yards rather than public parks, some want more police protection, fire protection, or cleaner streets."[15] Further, there is no *necessary* relationship between the nature of governmental organization in the metropolis on the one hand, and fiscal resources and service levels on the other. Core cities, which seemingly suffer the most from the principle of economic disparities, receive considerable monies from the state and federal governments; if central cities cannot provide minimum service levels due to inadequate fiscal resources, state and federal financial aid should be expanded to these units. In a normative sense, ensuring a *minimal* level of services throughout the region should be the collective responsibility of the state and federal levels of government; this responsibility should not be borne by the inhabitants of the region.

Finally, the adoption of metropolitan government would serve to further alienate the urban citizenry from government and the political process; as James Coleman and others have advanced, political alienation is one of the major problems found in the metropolis.[16] Reflective of this, as noted earlier, several scholars of urban affairs have called for the decentralization of service delivery systems and policy-making.[17] Dahl notes that civic participation is inversely associated with the population size of the political unit:

> The essential point is that nothing can overcome the dismal fact that as the number of citizens increases the proportion who can participate *directly* in discussions with their top leaders must necessarily grow smaller and smaller. The

inherent constraint is neither evil man nor evil institutions,
nor any other eradicable aspect of human life, but rather a
dimension of all existence that is morally neutral, because it
is implacable, unswearing, and inescapable-time.[18]

Mindful of the need of vigorous civic participation, Dahl
concludes that the *optimum* size for a contemporary
American city should be between 50,000 and 200,000
inhabitants.[19] This population range, of course, is hardly
conducive to the concept of metropolitan government. In a
somewhat similar fashion, Bish notes: "If anything, the
recent emphasis on alienation in the United States indicates
that perhaps smaller, rather than larger, political units are
needed to satisfy individual preferences."[20] We might add
that special districts and authorities are quite satisfactory
mechanisms for delivering those public services, like mass
transportation, that must be provided on a regional basis.[21]

## Councils of Governments:
### The Preferred Approach

At least from my perspective, consolidated metropolitan government is neither needed nor desirable for
American metropolitan areas. What is needed is a responsible and democratic mechanism for regional program coordination, policy direction, and management; and, this need
is met by councils of governments. I will not repeat here the
several achievements and accomplishments of councils;
however, we should also note the advantages of the
council-of-governments approach. First, councils do provide a *neutral* political arena where like public officials can
converse about common problems and negotiate regional
policies to deal with these problems. Second, councils are
relatively easy to organize; indeed, this study has found
that they are usually formed by an ardent and dedicated
few. Third, councils have the quality of being flexible in
organizational character. For example, state boundaries

are not an obstacle to council membership. Some councils of governments, like the Head of the Lakes Council of Governments,[22] of the Duluth, Minnesota/Superior, Wisconsin metropolitan area and the Metropolitan Washington Council of Governments (COG), have members from several states. In other instances, councils have encountered no difficulty in including in their membership peculiar but seemingly necessary members. The inclusion of the state of Oregon in the Mid-Willamette Valley Council of Governments (M-WVCOG) is but one testimony to this. And finally, the council-of-governments device is attractive because it is politically feasible; it does gain the approval of most of the elected officials of the metropolitan region.

What can be stated with regard to the current and future role of councils of governments in the metropolitan political world? It is evident that councils will remain a permanent feature of the American metropolis. This is simply so because these organizations have demonstrated their worth and utility; they have convinced many that they are a valuable political structure in the urban area. In short, councils have done the act of the politically possible; they have brought some measure of regionalism to the public sector of the American metropolis.

In summary, we should expect that in the immediate future the activities and functional concerns of councils will generally be essentially the same as presently constituted, although it is quite possible these bodies may gain added regional review powers and responsibilities. In *several* instances, councils might conceivably evolve into limited metropolitan governments with various functional responsibilities. But this will be a limited development given the strong antimetropolitan governmental attitude and tradition found in the American polity. However, in reality, the future of councils of governments will be decided by local officials and federal and state policies.

# Notes

1. Melvin B. Mogulof, *Governing Metropolitan Areas: A Critical Review of Councils of Governments and the Federal Role* (Washington, D.C.: The Urban Institute, 1971), p. 74.
2. Ibid., p. 114.
3. Atlanta Regional Commission, *Bylaws Atlanta Regional Commission* (Atlanta: The Commission, 1973).
4. Advisory Commission on Intergovernmental Relations, *Regional Decision Making: New Strategies for Substate Districts* (Washington, D.C.: The Commission, 1973), pp. 371-374. Regarding this recommendation, see also the following articles written by individuals associated with the Commission: Robert E. Merriam, "State-Designated Districts and Local Modernization," *National Civic Review* 63 (February 1974): 67-71; and David B. Walker and Carl W. Stenberg, "A Substate Districting Strategy," *National Civic Review* 63 (January 1974): 5-9, 15.
5. For information regarding the Metropolitan Council of Minneapolis-St. Paul, see Stanley Baldinger, *Planning and Governing the Metropolis* (New York: Praeger, 1971), and, John Fischer, "The Minnesota Experiment: How to Make a Big City Fit to Live In," *Harper's*, April 1969, pp. 12, 17-18, 20, 24, 26, 28, 30, 32.
6. Dale Rogers Marshall, "Metropolitan Government: Views of Minorities," in *Minority Perspectives*, ed. Lowdon Wingo (Washington, D.C.: Resources for the Future, 1972), p. 16.
7. Robert Wood, *Suburbia: Its People and Their Politics* (Boston: Houghton Mifflin, 1959).
8. Charles E. Lindblom, *The Intelligence of Democracy* (New York: The Free Press, 1965), p. 3.
9. Vincent Ostrom, Charles M. Tiebout, and Robert Warren, "The Organization of Government in Metropolitan Areas: A Theoretical Inquiry," *American Political Science Review* 55 (December 1961): 831-842.
10. H. Paul Friesema, *Metropolitan Political Structure: Intergovernmental Relations and Political Integration in the Quad Cities* (Iowa City: University of Iowa Press, 1971).
11. Brett Hawkins and Thomas R. Dye, "Metropolitan 'Fragmentation': A Research Note," *American Behavioral Scientist* 5 (May 1962): 11.

12. Alan Campbell and Seymour Sacks, *Metropolitan America: Fiscal Patterns and Governmental Systems* (New York: The Free Press, 1967), p. 179.

13. Robert Dahl, "The City in the Future of Democracy," *American Political Science Review* 61 (December 1967): 965-966.

14. Robert L. Bish and Vincent Ostrom, *Understanding Urban Government: Metropolitan Reform Reconsidered* (Washington, D.C.: American Enterprise Institute for Public Policy Research, 1973), p. 76.

15. Robert L. Bish, *The Public Economy of Metropolitan Areas* (Chicago: Markham Publishing Company, 1971), p. 153.

16. *Richmond Times-Dispatch,* 8 June 1975, p. F-7.

17. See Alan A. Altshuler, *Community Control: The Black Demand for Participation in Large American Cities* (New York: Pegasus, 1970), and Milton Kotler, *Neighborhood Government: The Local Foundations of Political Life* (New York: Bobbs-Merrill, 1969).

18. Dahl, "The City in the Future of Democracy," p. 957.

19. Ibid., p. 965.

20. Bish, *The Public Economy of Metropolitan Areas,* p. 155.

21. I am mindful, of course, that scholars of urban politics have generally been critical of the establishment and proliferation of special districts; however, in view of the evidence, perhaps it is time we reassess the value and utility of these bodies. For as Bish notes: ". . . Special districts play an important role in solving problems efficiently." See ibid., p. 68.

22. I was reminded of the interstate character of the Head of the Lakes Council of Governments by Richard Cihoski, Executive Secretary, in interview, August 22, 1974.

# Appendix

## *Individuals Interviewed*

Walter Aston, Chairman, Capitol Region Council of Elected Officials, Hartford, Connecticut, August 10, 1967.

Glenn E. Bennett, Secretary, Metropolitan Atlanta Council of Local Governments, Atlanta, June 13, 1967.

Richard Cihoski, Executive Secretary, head of the Lakes Council of Governments, Duluth, Minnesota, August 22, 1974.

Gerard H. Coleman, Executive Director, Supervisors' Inter-County Committee, Detroit, June 16, 1967.

Dana Hansen, Manager of Regional Development, Greater Hartford Chamber of Commerce, Hartford, Connecticut, August 8, 1967.

Chester A. Kunz, Executive Director, Regional Conference of Elected Officials, Philadelphia, June 6, 1967.

Kent Mathewson, President, Metropolitan Fund (formerly city administrator, Salem, Oregon), Detroit, June 15, 1967.

Walter Scheiber, Executive Director, Metropolitan Washington Council of Governments, Washington, D.C., June 8, 1967 and November 27, 1974.

James Thomas, information service officer, Southeast Michigan Council of Governments, (telephone interview), July 24, 1975.

Ralph Webster, Director of Administration, National Association of Regional Councils, Washington, D.C., June 20, 1974.

Harry West, Executive Director, Atlanta Regional Commission, Atlanta, November 6, 1974.

# Bibliography

*Books*

Altshuler, Alan. *Community Control: The Black Demand for Participation in Large American Cities.* New York: Pegasus, 1970.

Aron, Joan B. *The Quest for Regional Cooperation: A Study of the New York Metropolitan Regional Council.* Berkeley: University of California Press, 1969.

Baldinger, Stanley. *Planning and Governing the Metropolis: The Twin Cities' Experience.* New York: Praeger, 1971.

Banfield, Edward C. *The Unheavenly City Revisited.* Boston: Little, Brown and Company, 1974.

Bish, Robert L. *The Public Economy of Metropolitan Areas.* Chicago: Markham Publishing Company, 1971.

_____ and Ostrom, Vincent. *Understanding Urban Government: Metropolitan Reform Reconsidered.* Washington, D.C.: American Enterprise Institute for Public Policy Research, 1973.

Bollens, John C., ed. *Exploring the Metropolitan Community*. Berkeley: University of California Press, 1961.

_____ and Schmandt, Henry J. *The Metropolis: Its People, Politics, and Economic Life*. New York: Harper and Row, 1965.

Booth, David. *Metropolitics: The Nashville Consolidation*. East Lansing: Institute for Community Development and Services, Michigan State University, 1963.

Campbell, Alan, and Sacks, Seymour. *Metropolitan America: Fiscal Patterns and Governmental Services*. New York: The Free Press, 1967.

Frieden, Bernard J. *Metropolitan America: Challenge to Federalism*. Washington, D.C.: Advisory Commission on Intergovernmental Relations, 1966.

Friesema, H. Paul. *Metropolitan Political Structure: Intergovernmental Relations and Political Integration in the Quad-Cities*. Iowa City: University of Iowa Press, 1971.

Gordon, Mitchell. *Sick Cities: Psychology and Pathology of American Urban Life*. Baltimore: Penguin Books, 1963.

Graves, W. Brooks. *American Intergovernmental Relations*. New York: Scribner's, 1964.

Greer, Scott. *Governing the Metropolis*. New York: Wiley, 1962.

_____ *Metropolitics: A Study of Political Culture*. New York: Wiley, 1963.

Gulick, Luther. *The Metropolitan Problem and American Ideas*. New York: Knopf, 1962.

Havard, William C. and Floyd L. Corty. *Rural-Urban Consolidation*. Baton Rouge: Louisiana State University Press. 1964.

Hawley, Amos H. and Basil G. Zimmer. *The Metropolitan Community: Its People and Government*. Beverly Hills, Calif.: Sage Publications, 1970.

Jones, Victor. *Metropolitan Government.* Chicago: University of Chicago Press, 1942.

Kaplan, Harold. *Urban Political Systems: A Functional Analysis of Metro Toronto.* New York: Columbia University Press, 1967.

Kotler, Milton. *Neighborhood Government: The Local Foundations of Political Life.* New York: Bobbs-Merrill, 1969.

Lindblom, Charles E. *The Intelligence of Democracy: Decision Making Through Mutual Adjustment.* New York: Free Press, 1965.

Martin, Richard A. *Consolidation: Jacksonville-Duval County.* Jacksonville: Crawford Publishing Co., 1968.

Martin, Roscoe. *Metropolis in Transition: Local Government Adaptation to Changing Urban Needs.* Washington, D.C.: Government Printing Office, 1963.

Milbrath, Lester. *Political Participation.* Chicago: Rand McNally, 1965.

Mogulof, Melvin B. *Governing Metropolitan Areas: A Critical Review of Councils of Governments and the Federal Role.* Washington, D.C.: The Urban Institute, 1971.

Norton, James A. *The Metro Experience.* Cleveland: Western Reserve University Press, 1963.

Schmandt, Henry J.; Steinbecker, Paul G.; and Wendel, George. *Metropolitan Reform in St. Louis.* New York: Holt, Rinehart, and Winston, 1961.

Sofen, Edward. *The Miami Metropolitan Experiment.* Bloomington: Indiana University Press, 1963.

Studenski, Paul. *The Government of Metropolitan Areas.* New York: National Municipal League, 1930.

Warren, Robert O. *Government in Metropolitan Regions: A Reappraisal of Fractionated Political Organization.* Davis: Institute of Governmental Affairs, University of California, Davis, 1966.

Wirt, Frederick M. *Power in the City: Decision Making in*

*San Francisco.* Berkeley: University of California Press, 1974.

Wood, Robert. *Suburbia: Its People and Their Politics.* Boston: Houghton Mifflin, 1959.

———. *1400 Governments.* Garden City, N.Y.: Doubleday, Anchor Books, 1964.

Zimmerman, Joseph F. *The Federated City: Community Control in Large Cities.* New York: St. Martin's Press, 1972.

# Monographs

American Society of Planning Officials. *Voluntary Metropolitan Governmental Councils.* Chicago: The Society, 1962.

Bosworth, Karl A., and Wikstrom, Nelson. *Regional Councils of Elected Officials in Connecticut.* Storrs: Institute of Urban Research, The University of Connecticut, 1966.

Council of State Governments. *Coming Together: The Intergovernmental Cooperation Act of 1968 - Survey of Federal and State Implementation.* Washington, D.C.: The Council, 1971.

Douglas, Peter. *The Southern California Association of Governments: A Response to Federal Concern for Metropolitan Areas.* Los Angeles: Institute of Government and Public Affairs, University of California, 1968.

Frankel, Laurie, and Scheiber, Walter A. "Characteristics and Administrative Relationships of Regional Council Directors." In *Urban Data Service.* Washington, D.C.: International City Management Association, 1973.

Hanson, Royce. *The Politics of Metropolitan Coopera-*

*tion: Metropolitan Washington Council of Govern-
ments.* Washington, D.C.: Washington Center for
Metropolitan Studies, 1964.

———— *Metropolitan Councils of Governments.* Washington, D.C.: Advisory Commission on Intergovernmental Relations, 1966.

Harman, B. Douglas. "Areawide Review of Federal Grant
Applications: Implications for Urban Management."
In *Urban Data Service.* Washington, D.C.: Interna-
tional City Management Association, 1972.

Harris, Charles. *Regional COG's and the Central City.*
Detroit: Metropolitan Fund, 1970.

Institute for Local Self Government. *ABAG Appraised: A
Quinquennial Review of Voluntary Regional Cooper-
ative Action Through the Association of Bay Area
Governments.* Berkeley: Institute for Local Self
Government, 1965. Also 2d ed., 1967.

Johnson, Tobe. *Metropolitan Government: A Black
Analytical Perspective.* Washington, D.C.: Joint Center for Political Studies, 1972.

Mars, David. *The Formation of SCAG: A Case History.*
Los Angeles: School of Public Administration, University of Southern California, 1966.

Metropolitan Washington Council of Governments. *Councils of Governments.* Washington, D.C.: The Council,
1966.

———— *Goals, Objectives, and Work Program for Greater
Washington: An Overall Program Design for the
Metropolitan Washington Council of Governments,
1974-1976.* Washington, D.C.: The Council, 1974.

———— *Beyond the Handshake* . . . Washington, D.C.:
The Council, 1974.

National Association of Regional Councils. *Action
Through Intergovernmental Cooperation.* Washington, D.C.: The Council, 1972.

_____ *Special Report.* Washington, D.C.: The Association, 1972.

National Service to Regional Councils. *Regionalism: A New Dimension in Local Government and Intergovernmental Relations.* Washington, D.C.: The Service, 1971.

Small, Joseph F. *Governmental Alternatives Facing the Chicago Metropolitan Area.* Chicago: Center for Research in Urban Government, Loyola University, 1966.

The Texas Research League. *Metropolitan Texas: A Workable Approach to Its Problems.* Austin: Texas Research League, 1967.

## Reports

Committee for Economic Development. *Guiding Metropolitan Growth.* A Report Prepared by the Research and Policy Committee and Area Development Committee. New York: The Committee, 1960.

_____ *Modernizing Local Government.* A Report Prepared by the Research and Policy Committee. New York: The Committee, 1966.

_____ *Reshaping Government in Metropolitan Areas.* A Report Prepared by the Research and Policy Committee. New York: The Committee, 1970.

Committee of One Hundred. *Final Report: A Proposal for a Voluntary Council of Governments in Southeast Michigan.* Detroit: The Committee, 1966.

Metropolitan Atlanta Council of Local Governments. *MACLOG: 1966 Annual Report.* Atlanta: The Council, 1966.

Metropolitan Washington Council of Governments. *Report for 1966.* Washington, D.C.: The Council, 1966.

Mid-Willamette Valley Council of Governments and the Mid-Willamette Valley Planning Council. *Regional*

*Planning and Governmental Coordination.* A Report Prepared by Wesley M. Howe and Wesley J. Kvarsten. Salem, Ore.: Mid-Willamette Valley Council of Governments and the Mid-Willamette Valley Planning Council, 1967.

National Association of Regional Councils. *Regional Council Directory.* Washington, D.C.: The Association, 1973.

Southern California Association of Governments. *Annual Report '73.* Los Angeles: The Association, 1973.

## Public Documents

U.S., Advisory Commission on Intergovernmental Relations. *Factors Affecting Voter Reactions to Governmental Reorganization in Metropolitan Areas.* Washington, D.C.: The Commission, 1962.

———— *Performance of Urban Functions: Local and Area Wide.* Washington, D.C.: The Commission, 1963.

———— *Regional Decision Making: New Strategies for Substate Districts.* Washington, D.C.: The Commission, 1973.

U.S., Bureau of the Census. *Census of Governments, 1972 Government Organization.* Volume 1. Washington, D.C.: Government Printing Office, 1973.

U.S., Executive Office of the President, Bureau of the Budget. "Section 204 of the Demonstration Cities and Metropolitan Development Act of 1966: Two Years' Experience." Mimeographed. Washington, D.C.: The Bureau, 10 April 1970.

## Articles

Adrian, Charles R. "The Community Setting." In *Social Science and Community Action,* edited by Charles R.

Adrian, pp. 1-8. East Lansing: Michigan State University, 1960.

"Area Governments Join," *Public Management* 42 (November 1960): 258.

Baker, David L. "Case History of Southern California Association of Governments." In *Minutes of the AMA-NACO Workshop on Regional Cooperation,* pp. 19-21. Washington, D.C.: National Association of Counties, 1964.

Banfield, Edward C. "The Politics of Metropolitan Area Organization." *Midwest Journal of Political Science* 1 (May 1957): 77-91.

Barnes, Philip W. "Experience in Texas." *Midwest Review of Public Administration* 5 (February 1971): 39-42.

"Bay Area Council Adopts Representation by Population." *Metropolitan Area Digest* 10 (November-December 1967): 3.

"Bay Area Governments Propose a Regional Government." *Metropolitan Area Digest* 10 (January-February 1967): 5.

"Bay Area Unit Votes Association." *Metropolitan Area Problems* 3 (May-June 1960): 1.

Becker, Don. "Local Groups Study Metropolitan Seattle." *National Municipal Review* 43 (June 1954): 312-314.

Beckman, Norman. "Alternative Approaches for Metropolitan Reorganization." *Public Management* 46 (June 1964): 128-131.

_____. "Federal Policy for Metropolitan Governance." *National Civic Review* 63 (March 1974): 128-132.

Bellish, Jewell. Review of *Government in Metropolitan Areas: A Reappraisal of Fractionated Political Organization,* by Robert O. Warren. *National Civic Review* 56 (February, 1967): 119.

Bodine, John W. "Local Government Cooperation—Solution to Metropolis." *Public Management* 43 (October 1961): 226.

Bollens, John C. "Metropolitan and Fringe Area Developments in 1962." In *Municipal Year Book,* pp. 45-59. Chicago: International City Managers' Association, 1963.

––––––– "Metropolitan and Fringe Area Developments in 1963." In *Municipal Year Book,* pp. 52-68. Chicago: International City Managers' Association, 1964.

––––––– "Metropolitan and Fringe Area Developments in 1964." In *Municipal Year Book,* pp. 54-67. Chicago: International City Managers' Association, 1965.

––––––– "Metropolitan and Fringe Area Developments in 1965." In *Municipal Year Book,* pp. 55-65. Chicago: International City Managers' Association, 1966.

Bosley, John J. "A New Mechanism for Metropolitan Decision Making: Metropolitan Councils of Government," *American Bar Association Journal* 52 (January 1966): 90-91.

Bradley, Thomas. "Regional Governance and Racial and Ethnic Minorities." In *The Regionalist Papers,* edited by Kent Mathewson, pp. 163-173. Detroit: Metropolitan Fund, 1974.

Carrell, Jeptha. "Learning to Work Together." *National Municipal Review* 43 (November 1954): 526-533.

Cassella, William N., Jr. "Salem Citizens' Conference Reports." *National Civic Review* 49 (January 1960): 30-32.

––––––– "ABAG Adopts Statement of Principles." *National Civic Review* 51 (January 1962): 35.

––––––– "Air Pollution Control Stressed by RCEO." *National Civic Review* 51 (May 1962): 275-279.

––––––– "ABAG Suggested As Area Planning Agency." *National Civic Review* 51 (November 1962): 573.

––––––– "Local Governments Cooperate on Problems." *National Civic Review* 52 (April 1963): 213-214.

––––––– "Action Blueprint Presented to ABAG." *National Civic Review* 52 (May 1963): 275-276.

————. "Plan New California Agency for Regional Problems." *National Civic Review* 52 (July 1963): 384-385.

————. "San Francisco Enters ABAG." *National Civic Review* 53 (June 1964): 327-328.

————. "ABAG to Develop Regional Solutions." *National Civic Review* 53 (December 1964): 606-607.

————. "Town Meeting Held in Greater Hartford." *National Civic Review* 54 (January 1965): 36-38.

————. "Capital Area Group Seeks a Charter." *National Civic Review* 54 (March 1965): 155-156.

————. "COG Achieves Corporate Status." *National Civic Review* 54 (July 1965): 378.

————. "Regional Approach Stressed in Connecticut." *National Civic Review* 55 (April 1966): 212-213.

Cassella, William N., Jr., and Jones, Victor. "Area-Wide Council Proposed in Seattle." *National Municipal Review* 45 (September 1956): 396-398.

————. "Intercounty Committee Authorized for Michigan." *National Municipal Review* 46 (November 1957): 530.

Citizens Advisory Committee, Joint Committee on Urban Development, Legislature of the State of Washington, "Too Many Governments." In *Metropolitan Politics,* edited by Michael Danielson, pp. 127-135. Boston: Little, Brown and Co., 1966.

Citizens Research Council of Michigan. "Southeast Michigan Regionalism." In *The Regionalist Papers,* edited by Kent Mathewson, pp. 56-69. Detroit: Metropolitan Fund, 1974.

Coin, Richard M. "Accommodation Par Excellence: The Lakewood Plan." In *Metropolitan Politics,* edited by Michael N. Danielson, pp. 272-280. Boston: Little, Brown and Co., 1966.

Coke, James G. "The Objectives of Metropolitan Study," In *Metropolitan Analysis,* edited by Stephen B. Sweeney and George S. Blair, pp. 19-29. Philadelphia: University of Pennsylvania Press, 1958.

———. "Stability and Change: Local Government in the Philadelphia Metropolitan Area." *Public Administration Review* 23 (September 1963): 186-191.

Coleman, Gerard H. "Local Officials Find Cooperation Works." *National Civic Review* 51 (January 1962): 31-34.

"Computers Show What They Can Do for Law Enforcement." *Georgia Municipal Journal* 16 (February 1966): 15.

"Connecticut Capitol Region Organizes Council of Elected Officials." *Metropolitan Area Digest* 9 (March-April 1966): 5.

Connery, Robert H., and Leach, Richard H. "Southern Metropolis: Challenge to Government." *Journal of Politics* 26 (February 1964): 60-81.

Cox, James L. "Federal Urban Development Policy and the Metropolitan Washington Council of Governments: A Reassessment." *Urban Affairs Quarterly* 3 (September 1967): 75-94.

Cronin, Thomas E. "Metropolity Models and City Hall." *American Institute of Planners' Journal* 36 (May 1970): 189-197.

Dahl, Robert. "The City in the Future of Democracy." *American Political Science Review* 61 (December 1967): 953-970.

Dye, Thomas R. "Urban Political Integration: Conditions Associated with Annexation in American Cities." *Midwest Journal of Political Science* 8 (November 1964): 430-445.

Fales, James M., Jr. "Bay Area Cities, Counties Organize." *National Civic Review* 49 (October 1960): 491-493.

Finlayson, Judith. "Councils of Governments: What and Why Are They?" *American County Government* 32 (April 1967): 20-25.

"Fischer Cities Role of Regional Co-op Councils." *Metropolitan Area Problems* 6 (September-October 1963): 3-4.

Fischer, John. "The Minnesota Experiment: How to Make a Big City Fit to Live In." *Harper's,* 1 April 1969, p. 12, 17-18, 20, 24, 26, 28, 30, 32.

Francois, Francis B. "Who Will Make Our Regional Decisions?" *Nation's Cities* 10 (November 1972): 12.

Friedland, L. L. "Counties Cooperate in Detroit Area." *National Municipal Review* 46 (January 1957): 34-36.

Gable, William R. "The Metropolitan Council as a Device to Foster and Coordinate Intergovernmental Cooperation." In *Regional Organization,* part II, pp. 95-108. Detroit: Metropolitan Fund, 1965.

Gansel, Jean. "Regional Council Directors: Perspectives of External Influence." In *The Municipal Year Book, 1974,* pp. 50-56. Washington D.C.: International City Management Association, 1974.

———— and Stenberg, Carl W. "Regional Council Performance: The City Perspective." In *The Municipal Year Book, 1973,* pp. 63-76. Washington, D.C.: International City Management Association, 1973.

Garmen, Stephen L. "COGs '72: A Central City View: Coordination Instead of Competition." *Nation's Cities* 10 (November 1972): 28.

Gleason, James P. "COGs '72: A Suburban View." *Nation's Cities* 10 (November 1972): 29.

Grant, Daniel R. "Urban and Suburban Nashville: A Case Study in Metropolitanism." *Journal of Politics* 17 (February 1955): 82-99.

———— "Metropolitics and Professional Political Leadership: The Case of Nashville." *Annals of the American Academy of Political and Social Science* 353 (May 1964): 72-83.

Gulick, Luther. "Metropolitan Organization." *Annals of*

*the American Academy of Political and Social Science* 314 (November 1957): 57-65.

Hanson, Royce. "Federal Aid Spurs Area Councils." *National Civic Review* 55 (July 1966): 401-403.

Harmon, B. Douglas. "Councils of Governments and Metropolitan Decision-Making." In *Municipal Year Book, 1969,* pp. 10-16. Washington, D.C.: International City Management Association, 1969.

Hartman, Richard C. "Massive Cooperation—The Next Step?" *Western City* 35 (January 1959): 18-22.

_____ "The State's Role in Regionalism," In *The Regionalist Papers,* edited by Kent Mathewson, pp. 236-253. Detroit: Metropolitan Fund, 1974.

Harris, Charles. "Blacks and Regionalism: Councils of Governments." *National Civic Review* 62 (May 1973): 254-258.

Hawkins, Brett. "Public Opinion and Metropolitan Reorganization in Nashville." *Journal of Politics* 28 (May 1966): 408-418.

Hawkins, Brett, and Dye, Thomas R. "Metropolitan 'Fragmentation': A Research Note." *American Behavioral Scientist* 5 (May 1962): 11.

Hoadley, Wyn N. "Metropolitan Councils: The St. Louis Experience." *National Civic Review* 60 (February 1971): 79-85.

Howels, Wesley M. "Mid-Willamette Valley of Oregon Forms Council of Governments." *Western City* 42 (March 1966): 23-26.

Humes, Samuel. "Washington Area Reports Progress." *National Civic Review* 50 (November 1961): 550-552.

_____ "Organization for Metropolitan Cooperation." *Public Management* 44 (May 1962): 105-107.

Hutchison, Claude B. "Metropolitan Council Proposed in Bay Area." *Western City* 36 (June 1960): 23.

Jones, Victor. "Local Government Organization in

Metropolitan Areas: Its Relation to Urban Redevelopment," part IV. In *The Future of Cities and Urban Redevelopment,* edited by Coleman Woodbury, pp. 476-606. Chicago: University of Chicago Press, 1953.

————. "Cooperative Pattern." *National Civic Review* 51 (June 1962): 302-308.

Kammerer, Gladys M. "The Politics of Metropolis: Still a Frontier." *Public Administration Review* 23 (December 1963): 240-246.

Leach, Richard H. "New Urban Challenge." *National Civic Review* 50 (October 1961): 480-484.

Levenson, Rosaline. "Hartford Considers Regional Agencies." *National Civic Review* 55 (November 1966): 591-593.

"Local Governments Forming Regional Councils." *Public Management* 42 (July 1960): 155.

Long, Allen. "Creative Self-Help Marks the D.C. Area's Council of Governments." *Commonwealth* 37 (July 1970): 36-41.

Long, Norton. "Politics and Planning," In *The Polity,* edited by Charles Press, pp. 192-195. Chicago: Rand McNally and Company, 1962.

Maier, Henry W. "Conflict in Metropolitan Areas." *The Annals of the American Academy of Political and Social Science* 416 (November 1974): 148-157.

Marando, Vincent L. "Metropolitan Research and Councils of Governments." *Midwest Review of Public Administration* 5 (February 1971): 3-15.

————. "Voting in City-County Consolidation." *Western Political Quarterly* 26 (March 1973): 90-96.

————. "The Politics of City-County Consolidation." *National Civic Review* 64 (February 1975): 76-81.

Marshall, Dale Rogers. "Metropolitan Government: Views of Minorities," In *Minority Perspectives,* edited by

Lowdon Wingo, pp. 9-30. Washington, D.C.: Resources for the Future, 1972.

Mathewson, Kent. "Recommendations Made for Intergovernmental Cooperation." *Public Management* 42 (January 1960): 11.

_____ "Blueprint for Regional Cooperation." *Mayor and Manager* 4 (March 1961): 4-6.

_____ "A Growing Movement." *National Civic Review* 57 (June 1968): 298-302.

_____ "A Regional Ethic," In *The Regionalist Papers,* edited by Kent Mathewson, pp. 41-51. Detroit: Metropolitan Fund, 1974.

Mauldin, Douglas B. "Puget Group Reports Progress." *National Civic Review* 51 (May 1962): 272-274.

McCandless, Carl A. "Metro Charter Campaign Fails." *National Civic Review* 49 (February 1960): 91-93.

Merriam, Robert E. "State-Designated Districts and Local Modernization." *National Civic Review* 63 (February 1974): 67-71.

"Metro Officials Are Planning an Organization." *Georgia Municipal Journal* 14 (July 1964): 17.

"Metropol: Working Together for Better Law Enforcement." *Georgia Municipal Journal* 15 (September: 1965), 8-11.

"Metropolitan Washington Council Expands Activities." *Metropolitan Area Digest* 9 (July-August 1966): 4.

Mogulof, Melvin B. "Metropolitan Councils of Governments and the Federal Role." *Urban Affairs Quarterly* 7 (June 1972): 489-507.

Morgan, David R. "Attitudes Among Local Officials Toward a Council of Governments: The Oklahoma City Situation." *Midwest Review of Public Administration* 5 (February 1971): 36-39.

National Service to Regional Councils. "Coordination

Eliminates Conflicting Efforts." *Regional Review Quarterly* 4 (January 1971): 9.

_____. "Crime and Juvenile Delinquency: A Regional Problem." *Regional Review Quarterly* 4 (January 1971): 8, 16.

_____. "Faster Emergency Assistance Through Flexible Regional Councils." *Regional Review Quarterly* 4 (January 1971): 8.

_____. "Training Public Officials On a Regional Basis." *Regional Review Quarterly* 4 (January 1971): 14.

_____. "Wanted: Better Transportation Facilities." *Regional Review Quarterly* 4 (January 1971): 13.

_____. "Working for Clean Air and a Quality Environment." *Regional Review Quarterly* 4 (January 1971): 4.

Norton, James A. "Referenda Voting in a Metropolitan Area." *Western Political Quarterly* 16 (March 1963): 195-212.

Ostrom, Vincent; Tiebout, Charles M; and Warren, Robert. "The Organization of Government in Metropolitan Areas: A Theoretical Inquiry." *American Political Science Review* 55 (December 1961): 831-842.

Parker, John K. "Cooperation in Metropolitan Areas Through Councils of Governments." *Public Management* 45 (October 1963): 223-225.

Piven, Frances Fox, and Cloward, Richard A. "Black Control of Cities: Heading Off by Metropolitan Government." *New Republic,* 30 September 1967, pp. 19-21.

_____. "Black Control of Cities—II: How the Negroes Will Lose." *New Republic,* 7 October 1967, pp. 15-19.

"RCEO Receives Grant for Air Pollution Survey." *Metropolitan Area Digest* 9 (July-August 1966): 5.

"Regional Council Formed." *Public Management* 43 (October 1961): 232.

"Regional Group Organizes." *Public Management* 43 (May 1961): 114.

"Regional Programs Progress in Oregon—Cooperative Action Benefits Salem Area." *National Civic Review* 53 (May 1964): 264-266.

Rowlands, David D. "Governmental Cooperation Promotes Regional Planning." *Public Management* 42 (April 1960): 81.

"Salem Cooperation Shows Results." *Metropolitan Area Problems: News and Digest* 3 (July-August 1960): 3.

Salisbury, Robert H. "The Dynamics of Reform: Charter Politics in St. Louis." *Midwest Journal of Political Science* 5 (August 1960): 474-484.

Savage, Philip M. "How Philadelphia Fosters Intergovernmental Cooperation." *Nation's Cities* 2 (April 1964): 19-21.

Sayre, Wallace S., and Polsby, Nelson. "American Political Science and the Study of Urbanization." In *The Study of Urbanization,* edited by Philip M. Hauser and Leo F. Schnore, pp. 115-156. New York: Wiley, 1965.

Scheiber, Walter A. "A Council of Governments." *American City* 32 (May 1967): 110-112.

———. "Evolving a Policy Process for a Metropolitan Region." *Public Administration Review* 27 (September 1967): 258-261.

Schmandt, Henry J. "The Area Council-Approach to Metropolitan Government." *Public Management* 42 (February 1960): 30-32.

———. "The Emerging Strategy." *National Civic Review* 55 (June 1966): 325-330.

Scott, Stanley. "Bay Area Association Holds First

Meeting." *National Civic Review* 50 (April 1961): 202-206.

————. "Bay Area Association Reviews Year's Work." *National Civic Review* 51 (May 1962): 274-275.

Seyler, William C. "Interlocal Relations: Cooperation." *The Annals of the American Academy of Political and Social Science* 416 (November 1974): 158-169.

Sofen, Edward. "The Problems of Metropolitan Leadership: The Miami Experience." *Midwest Journal of Political Science* 5 (February 1961): 18-38.

"Southern California Officials Form Regional Council." *Metropolitan Area Problems* 9 (January-February 1966): 1.

Sparlin, Estal E. "Cleveland Seeks New Metro Solution." *National Civic Review* 49 (March 1960): 142-144.

Stephens, Ross. "Some Concluding Observations." *Midwest Review of Public Administration* 5 (February 1971): 47-49.

Studenski, Paul. "Metropolitan Areas 1960." *National Civic Review* 49 (October 1960): 467-473.

Tellenaar, Kenneth C. "Salem Area Stresses Massive Cooperation." *National Municipal Review* 47 (December 1958): 574-575.

"Unique Government Cooperation in Puget Sound Regional Transportation Study." *Western City* 38 (February 1962): 28.

Van Horn, Robert F. "Regional Programs Progress in Oregon." *National Civic Review* 53 (May 1964): 264-266.

Walker, David B., and Stenberg, Carl W. "A Substate Districting Strategy." *National Civic Review* 63 (January 1974): 5-9.

"Washington Council Seeks to Curb Air Pollution." *Metropolitan Area Digest* 9 (November-December 1966): 9.

Watson, Richard A., and Romani, John H. "Metropolitan

Government for Metropolitan Cleveland: An Analysis of the Voting Record." *Midwest Journal of Political Science* 5 (November 1961): 365-390.

Wikstrom, Nelson. "Councils of Governments." *Maine Townsman* 31 (June 1969): 5-6.

———— "Attitudes Toward COGs in Connecticut." *Midwest Review of Public Administration* 5 (February 1971): 42-44.

Willbern, York. "Unigov: Local Government Reorganization in Indianapolis." In *The Regionalist Papers,* edited by Kent Mathewson, pp. 207-229. Detroit: Metropolitan Fund, 1974.

Wood, Robert C. "A Division of Powers in Metropolitan Areas." In *Area and Power,* edited by Arthur Maass, pp. 53-69. Glencoe, Ill.: The Free Press, 1959.

Woodbury, Coleman. "The Background and Prospects of Urban Redevelopment in the United States," part V. In *The Future of Cities and Urban Redevelopment* edited by Coleman Woodbury, pp. 611-758. Chicago: University of Chicago Press, 1953.

Zimmerman, Joseph F. "Metropolitan Ecumenism: The Road to the Promised Land?" *Journal of Urban Law* 44 (Spring 1967): 433-457.

———— "The Planning Riddle." *National Civic Review* 57 (April 1968): 189-194.

———— "Metropolitan Reform in the U.S.: An Overview." *Public Administration Review* 30 (September/October 1970): 531-543.

———— Substate Regional Government: Designing a New Procedure." *National Civic Review* 61 (June 1972): 286-290.

———— "Meeting Service Needs Through Intergovernmental Agreements." In *The Municipal Year Book 1973,* pp. 79-88. Washington, D.C.: International City Management Association, 1973.

———— "The Metropolitan Area Problem." *The Annals of*

*the American Academy of Political and Social Science*
416 (November 1974): 133-147.

## Unpublished Materials

Association of Bay Area Governments, *ABAG*. Berkeley:
The Association, 1974.

———— *Program Capsule: A-95 Review Function Promotes Cooperation among Governments*. Berkeley:
The Association, 1974.

Atlanta Regional Commission, *Bylaws Atlanta Regional
Commission*. Atlanta: The Commission, 1973.

Hanson, Royce. "The Council of Governments—What Is
It?" Paper presented at The First National Conference of Councils of Governments, Washington, D.C.,
2 April 1967. Mimeographed.

Miller, Robert G. "The Association of Bay Area Governments: Intergovernmental Relations at the Regional
Level." Statement to the Subcommittee on Intergovernmental Relations of the Committee on Government Operations of the United States Senate. Prepared by the Association. Berkeley: 1967.
Mimeographed.

———— "Regional Home Rule and Government of the San
Francisco Bay Area." Statement to the (California)
Assembly Committee on Municipal and County
Government Regarding Assembly Bill No. 50. Pre-
pared by the Association. Berkeley: 1967.
Mimeographed.

Muskie, Edmund S. "Leadership and Change in American
Government." Paper presented at The First National
Conference of Councils of Governments, Washington,
D.C., 4 April 1967. Mimeographed.

Puget Sound Governmental Conference. "Puget Sound
Governmental Conference: A Synopsis." Seattle: The
Conference, 1966. Mimeographed.

Romney, George. "Special Message on Local and Urban Affairs." Transmitted to the 74th Michigan Legislature, 31 March 1967. Mimeographed.

Weaver, Robert C. "The Emerging Growth of Urban Councils." Paper presented at The First National Conference of Councils of Governments, Washington, D.C., 3 April 1967. Mimeographed.

Wikstrom, Nelson. "Attitudes of Selected Political Actors in Connecticut Toward the Council of Governments Concept." Paper presented to the Maine Conference of Social Scientists, University of Maine, Orono, Maine, April 9, 1970. Mimeographed.

————. "Councils of Governments: A Review of Twenty Years." Paper presented at the 1975 National Conference on Public Administration, Chicago, April 1-4, 1975. Mimeographed.

## *Letters*

Bennett, Glenn E., executive director, Atlanta Region Metropolitan Planning Commission, to the author, 28 June 1967.

DeLuce, Louis S., Office of the Mayor, New Haven, to the author, 8 June 1967.

Meays, Barton R., deputy executive director, Southern California Association of Governments, to the author, 7 November 1974 and 6 August 1975.

Pelughoeft, Larry, assistant director, Governmental Services, Puget Sound Governmental Conference, to the author, 24 December 1974.

Scheiber, Walter A., executive director, Metropolitan Washington Council of Governments, to the author, 29 June 1967.

Takayesu, Frederick T., research associate, Puget Sound Governmental Conference, to the author, 27 July 1967.

## *Addresses*

Scheiber, Walter A., at The First National Conference of Councils of Governments, Washington, D.C., 2 April 1967.

Enruh, Jesse, at The University of Connecticut, 1 May 1967.

## *Newspapers*

Eisen, Jack. "COG Adds Action to 10 Years of Talk." *The Washington Post,* 11 April 1967.

*Hartford Courant,* 3 March, 13 March, 19 May, 14 July 1966; 25 May, 29 June, 30 June 1967; 17 January, 18 March 1968.

*Hartford Times,* 28 February, 2 March, 12 March, 24 March, 10 May, 14 July, 27 October, 1 December 1966; 20 July 1967.

*New York Times,* 17 November 1974.

*Philadelphia Bulletin,* 11 June, 2 July 1961; 2 November 1963; 11 May, 14 May 1964; 19 January 1966.

Phillips, Allen. "COG Moves Closer Despite Foes." *Detroit News,* 15 June 1967.

*Richmond Times-Dispatch,* 8 June 1975.

Spalding, Jack. "The Community Group Fills the Vacuum." *Atlanta Journal,* 18 September 1966.

*Washington Evening Star,* 15 December 1966.

*Washington Post,* 19 April 1973; 22 October 1974.

# Index

**Nelson Wikstrom** is not a desk-bound college professor, but one who gets into the field to gather his data first hand. His book is based in part on in-depth interviews conducted with elected officials, city and town managers, political party leaders and those associated with councils of governments.

Since 1975 he has been Associate Professor of Political Science at Virginia Commonwealth University, located in Richmond, where in addition to teaching courses in American government and urban politics, he conducts research projects. Prior to joining Virginia Commonwealth University, Professor Wikstrom was associated with the University of Wisconsin and the University of Maine.

He has contributed articles to the *Midwest Review of Public Administration, National Civic Review, Virginia Social Science Journal, and Maine Townsman,* and has written book reviews and notes for a number of professional journals.

Professor Wikstrom is a member of the American Political Science Association, Southern Political Science Association, American Society for Public Administration, National Municipal League, and the Virginia Social Science Association.

He completed his undergraduate work at Northeastern University and received his M.A. and Ph.D. degrees from the University of Connecticut.